Speak for Yourself

PEARSON

At Pearson, we believe in learning – all kinds of learning for all kinds of people. Whether it's at home, in the classroom or in the workplace, learning is the key to improving our life chances.

That's why we're working with leading authors to bring you the latest thinking and the best practices, so you can get better at the things that are important to you. You can learn on the page or on the move, and with content that's always crafted to help you understand quickly and apply what you've learned.

If you want to upgrade your personal skills or accelerate your career, become a more effective leader or more powerful communicator, discover new opportunities or simply find more inspiration, we can help you make progress in your work and life.

Pearson is the world's leading learning company. Our portfolio includes the Financial Times, Penguin, Dorling Kindersley, and our educational business, Pearson International.

Every day our work helps learning flourish, and wherever learning flourishes, so do people.

To learn more please visit us at: **www.pearson.com/uk**

Speak for Yourself

Talk to impress, influence and make an impact

Harry Key

Harlow, England • London • New York • Boston • San Francisco • Toronto • Sydney • Auckland • Singapore • Hong Kong
Tokyo • Seoul • Taipei • New Delhi • Cape Town • São Paulo • Mexico City • Madrid • Amsterdam • Munich • Paris • Milan

Pearson Education Limited
Edinburgh Gate
Harlow CM20 2JE
United Kingdom
Tel: +44 (0)1279 623623
Web: www.pearson.com/uk

First published 2014 (print and electronic)

© Key Impact Inc. Ltd 2014 (print and electronic)

Pearson Education is not responsible for the content of third party internet sites.

ISBN: 978-0-273-78538-5 (print)
978-0-273-78886-7 (PDF)
978-0-273-78885-0 (ePub)

British Library Cataloguing-in-Publication Data
A catalogue record for the print edition is available from the British Library

Library of Congress Cataloging-in-Publication Data
Key, Harry.
  Speak for Yourself : Talk to Impress, Influence and Make an Impact / Harry Key Pearson.
    pages cm
  Includes bibliographical references and index.
  ISBN 978-0-273-78538-5
1. Conversation analysis. 2. Oral communication. 3. Dialogue analysis. I. Title.
  P95.45.K49 2014
  302.3'46--dc23
                                    2013031323

10 9 8 7 6 5 4 3 2 1
17 16 15 14 13

Cover design by Two Associates Ltd
Cover image © trekandshoot/Alamy

Print edition typeset in 9/13pt Helvetica LT Pro by 30
Print edition printed and bound in Great Britain by Henry Ling Ltd., at the Dorset Press, Dorchester, Dorset

NOTE THAT ANY PAGE CROSS-REFERENCES REFER TO THE PRINT EDITION

Contents

About the author

Harry Key is a Provocative speech and confidence coach. After studying theatre in Australia, he went through a variety of transformations, one of which involved being a Bollywood actor and voice artist in India. While working as a voice artist, Harry developed a curiosity in how we relate to one another and present ourselves to the world – and a suspicion that humorous and direct approaches might be the key. He discovered Provocative Therapy from author and international trainer Sue Knight, and almost immediately left India and became a speech and confidence coach in London. He now runs a business which focuses on sharing performance skills and using humour to challenge people, giving them space to share their presence, and in turn, the confidence to challenge the people around them.

Introduction

Hello...

You want to speak well, and you want people to listen.

More than listen, you want to find a way of speaking that makes them understand, believe, and *act*. You'd like people to enjoy your company, to agree with you, and disagree with you in enjoyable ways. You'd like to have one of those voices that can sound certain while still being friendly and fun. You want to have a presence that affects people, that exudes authority and commands respect. You need this, because you've got some great ideas and it's important that they're heard.

This book is here to help you:

→ breathe, move and speak in ways that make you feel calm, happy and confident;

→ feel more confident in an increasing variety of situations;

→ think differently, about your own and other people's behaviour;

→ read and interpret the behaviour of others so you can be more persuasive and influential;

→ and *most importantly*, be a better speaker, in private, in public, anywhere.

This book is a test of itself: in teaching you how to become more persuasive, I must be very persuasive, explain myself clearly and convince you to join in and get the most out of it. For the bits that work better as audio or visual exercises, like the sound of speaking from your gut or nuances in body language, there are resources on the website www.pearson-books.com/speakforyourself.

These are marked with a key: **O━━➤**

These resources include links to video and audio that will make certain exercises clearer and more easy to follow; plus there's an expanding range of links to talks and articles about ideas which are relevant. Hopefully, in time, you too will share some of your own skills and ideas online, and continue to learn from others.

This book has a deliberate structure, with each idea and skill building upon those which precede it. You'll get the most out of it if you read it in order, from front to back, rather than jumping to bits which you think might be relevant. But, this book is yours now, so if you really wanted to, you could feed it to your dog (though if it's on an ereader, you might kill both in the process).

This book is divided into three sections: The Voice, The Words, and The Style.

The Voice

This section will, unsurprisingly, focus upon your voice. We'll look at your whole body as if it's your voice. We'll consider your posture, breathing, enunciation and inflection so that you can exude certainty, calmness or confidence whenever you choose. Most excitingly, you'll find that there are simple, scientifically supported changes you can make to the way you breathe, speak and hold yourself that will have a remarkable impact on how you feel about yourself, and how you are received by the people around you. The purpose of The Voice part is to develop your presence.

The Words

This will focus on the content of what you're saying. We'll look at persuasion, and how to match what you're saying and how you're saying it to fit better with whoever you're talking to. I'll talk about a phenomenon I call flow, which is a trance-like state of entrainment between people, how to recognise it, and how to induce it. We'll cover the importance of listening to people and using their words, on storytelling, and on speaking to people at their level in an engaging way to induce these states of flow. You'll enhance your persuasive power by developing a keen understanding of the people around you.

The Style

This part will focus on putting *you* back into what you're doing. Here, we'll go off script a bit because it's about defining yourself as an individual rather than conforming to an established norm. We'll look at how you can read people and interpret their behaviour, develop your leadership skills, and use humour to playfully provoke from people the kind of behaviour you want to see. It's about being confident and owning yourself and shaping your life, which encourages others to do the same. It comes from a method of psychotherapy that uses humour as a tool for change which I've adapted because I think it's pretty enjoyable and applicable to everyday life. I call it Provocative Style, and it may be where you start to notice that my ideas diverge from those of other people who write about this stuff. I recommend that, having learned all the 'rules', you then break them, and set about creating a way of being that works best for you. At times this approach is rude (if that works for you), at times it's shocking (ditto), but it's always a lot of fun and very, very effective.

By the end of this book, you should be able to speak in a way that you are heard, and heard in a way that makes people listen. You'll stand, walk, talk and interact with people with confidence, control and calmness. This way of being creates connections with people. You'll be an excellent listener and a compelling talker; you'll be funny, bold, and willing to challenge people to improve their lives so they may seek to improve the lives of others. I do realise that at this stage, that might sound a bit grand. If you picked up this book to become more comfortable speaking to groups or networking, or to become better at negotiating, you'll achieve that too.

These exercises and ideas will become more and more challenging; not due to an increasing level of difficulty, but because they'll be asking you to do increasingly strange things (usually in private, and always with a clear purpose). The aim is for you to soon find these strange things less and less strange, until you're left with a greater variety of ways to be. You will have a big voice when you need it, a fun voice, a joking voice, and a voice that makes people's pants fall down. You'll have a variety of ways of structuring messages, and a wider range of methods for interpreting the actions and words of others. With such an arsenal of behaviour and supporting ideas, you will feel comfortable and confident in an increasing variety of situations; when meeting new people, talking to groups, or asking your boss for a raise. You'll be able to adjust your behaviour down to its very core, from the way you breathe, to how you speak and where you access your voice (hint: it's in your guts!). You'll change what you say, how you say it and how you hold yourself. You'll invent new ways of being yourself but they will all be 'you'. These exercises may even change how you think and what you believe, about yourself, others, and the world around you.

You may be tempted to skip over some exercises, deciding that you don't need to do them and *imagining* instead what it'd be like if you had. Imagining is horrendously ineffective because you won't get the benefit. If you just imagine that you did it, you'll decide either that there was no benefit, or that you already have that benefit (but you won't, in much the same way that imagining having sex yields very different results to actually having it). If you're on a train or somewhere public, there may be some activities that you'll want to put aside and come back to later (again, not unlike sex). That's fine, but make sure you do – if you get too far ahead you'll be trying to build skills upon a foundation that does not yet exist. Even if you have already done these exercises, or already speak with a strong voice, and have a good posture and breathe well, if you skip parts, you'll miss out on the experience of being consciously aware of what happens within you and around you when you change how you behave. This awareness is vital because later in the book you'll be focusing on creating these calm, confident and comfortable states in others.

Read the ideas, reflect on them, and challenge them. There may be many you've already heard of, and some variations which you feel work better for you. I've drawn ideas from a wealth of life experience, from theatre and yogic practices to a structure for understanding and talking to people called Neuro-Linguistic Programming or NLP (with which I've attempted to distill the bullshit and focus on the brilliance). A lot of reading and research on human behaviour has gone into this, as well as a load of personal experiences in an attempt to make it more enjoyable to read. I may, on some of these ideas, be totally wrong (obviously I don't think I am, but who does think they're wrong?). If you disagree with something, use the methods with which you do agree to skillfully propose your own ideas. Speak about them. Write a blog, make a video. Share your ideas and test them. This is how we, as a species, evolve.

That's why I'm writing this book.

I want to give people effective ways of disagreeing with one another, of presenting their opinions in persuasive ways. I want people to challenge each other to adjust their beliefs and behaviour, and to do so effectively, with confidence, compassion and good humour.

Let's crack on, shall we?

The Voice

Part One

A beautiful voice is a powerful thing. A versatile voice can persuade, excite or intimidate; it can be intimate, impress or soothe. Before we can get onto the content of your speech or the style of your delivery, you need to gain a mindful awareness and control of your body. Your voice, as I think of it, is more than the pitch, volume and pace with which you speak – it is your whole being. Gain control of your deeper processes, breathe differently, mindfully, and you can project your voice from a place of power. It will not just affect how you are received, but also how you feel about yourself. Standing, speaking and moving differently will change your self-perception in ways that are quite amazing; so amazing that I've gone to some lengths to demonstrate to you that these ideas are well supported scientifically.

In this section we'll cover:

→ some of the techniques and vocal skills I've learned and developed;
→ some of the science and rationale behind breathing and posture;
→ breathing techniques to change how you breathe and where you speak from;
→ the importance of posture and how it affects the way you feel.

Breathe with your belly

Chapter One

In order to affect changes in others, we must be able to change ourselves. As you develop your skill for adjusting your physiology on a fundamental level, your emotions and thoughts will shift. Breathing well will dramatically alter your mental state, giving you access to calmer, happier thoughts; it will improve your physical wellbeing, your voice, and your general enjoyment of life. Influential people are invariably calm, confident and can be easily heard. When you breathe well, you'll feel this way too. When you use your stomach and diaphragm to speak, your voice will have a depth and power which will be quite compelling and easy to listen to. Doing so will give you a self-awareness and control that makes you adept at recognising and affecting the emotions, thoughts and actions of others.

In the paragraphs that follow, we'll run through some exercises that will help you build an awareness about how you currently breathe, and explain the benefits of breathing to the belly through your nose.

What do you mean 'bad at breathing'?

You are a remarkably complex organism. You have evolved, through billions of permutations, from something like sludge, into something that swam, into something that crawled; onwards and upwards into the attractive individual who now flexes and winks at you from the mirror each morning. To an attractive and infinitely evolved being such as yourself, it may seem strange to suggest that you could be 'bad' at something as basic as breathing. So consider this...

The act of sitting has become very common, very quickly. Our physiology has not evolved to handle quite so much of it. When you go camping, you're sampling a more primitive lifestyle, and you'll notice that it's difficult to find many good sitting logs that don't have offensive branches poking out at dangerous angles. Prehistoric humans lived that life. They spent most of their time walking around, squatting, or lying down, propped up on their elbows. Sitting, as you do now (on the train, in the car, at your desk, on the toilet, on a sofa, watching telly and probably even right now, reading this), is a radically new posture for the human frame. It only became *really* common when we enslaved ourselves to pecking at our computers endlessly. This pandemic sitting has struck within the blink of an evolutionary eye, and we just aren't built for it.

Sitting and slouching has caused our stomach muscles to let themselves go. Ideally, they'd be engaging constantly throughout the day, working with your back muscles to keep your torso upright as you twist and bend and arch, while gathering things, hunting things, and avoiding being eaten by the things hunting you. Now, when we sit and hunch, gravity and a chair back stop our torso from toppling backwards, and we're usually hunched forwards, allowing the tensile strain of the vertebrae and discs to stop our chin from resting on our knees. Our tummy muscles relax and let our guts flop forwards into a slack bag of belly. Ideally, when you inhale, the air entering your lungs will push your stomach out, but with a tummy that has expanded to its limit, there's nowhere for the guts to go. Many of us try to combat this ballooning belly syndrome by doing lots of sit-ups, but this can cause similar breathing problems for the opposite reasons. Many washboard stomachs are *too* toned, and between their strength and our vanity, they refuse to expand as we inhale. Fitties, fatties and computer slaves alike, most of us don't breathe with our bellies. Our upper chest takes up the role instead. After hundreds of millions of breaths, our muscles have been trained to ignore their evolutionary design, and it almost seems strange to suggest that it should be done differently. Particularly in the West, we have become a race of chest-breathers.

Take a deep breath, right now. Where does it go?

Do this:

Breathing awareness exercise

Wear clothes that will let you see what's happening to your chest and stomach as you breathe, and stand in front of a full-length mirror. Stand as you normally would. Just breathe for a few minutes. It's a rare thing, so enjoy it. Focus your attention on your breathing and as you watch yourself, bring a new awareness to the familiar and forgotten sensation of breathing.

Now think about each of the following questions.

→ How does the air come in and out: is it a smooth movement, or jagged and abrupt in parts?

▶

→ Do you breathe fast or slow? Are they long or short breaths?

→ Is the inhale and exhale of the same duration, or is one faster than the other?

Breathe again and consider these questions:

→ Is there a pause between inhale and exhale, or exhale and inhale?

→ Do you normally breathe through your nose or your mouth and nose? Many people normally mouth breathe, but when they pay attention, they breathe in through the nose and out through the mouth.

→ Watch your shoulders as you inhale: do they rise, stay still, drop, pull back or hunch forward?

→ Watch your stomach: does it push out on inhale or suck in? Does it move at all?

To accentuate the effect, take a deep breath and focus on all of the factors mentioned and see how it differs from your normal breathing. When you take a deep breath, which fills first, your chest or your stomach?

Depending on what you saw in the mirror during that exercise, you're either a bad breather or a good breather. Let's have a look at some of the traits for each.

Bad breathing

✗ As you inhale, your shoulders lift up and draw towards your ears like a small shrug.

✗ You usually breathe through your mouth (many of us naturally breathe through our mouths, but when we're conscious of it, we inhale through the nose).

✗ Upon inhale, your chest puffs out slightly.

✗ When you exhale, your shoulders drop to let the air out.

✗ When you take a deep breath, your shoulders raise right up and your stomach sucks in, and if you take more than three or four big breaths, you get dizzy and start seeing stars.

✗ Your breaths are quick, and jagged or uneven in parts, and you can hear them.

So, you found out you're a 'bad' breather: you breathe through your mouth, mostly into your chest, and you perhaps snore a bit at night and carry stress in your shoulders? Don't worry, except for people who've trained their breathing (through playing the sax, singing, yoga or drama classes), most of us are bad at breathing. Even those who are trained will often breathe badly unless they're thinking about it.

Why is it bad?

Chest breathing evolved for high intensity occasions, it's your turbo boost for when you are running from danger or punching it in the face. In those moments, your body will be on high alert, with adrenaline coursing through your veins and expanding your airways to draw more oxygen into your lungs. Your veins expand, as your heart rate speeds up, pushing torrents of oxygen-rich blood into muscles that need it for all the running and face-punching. Your pupils dilate to let in more light, in case the threat that needs punching or running from has crept up on you under cover of darkness. Your body is like a loaded trap. Your mind is a knife edge, primed to perceive threats, tiny sounds, glints of light or flashes of shadow and react to them as quickly as possible. At times like this, your higher-order processing is almost totally shut down (allowing you to act without wasting your time thinking). You won't write any poetry, chat calmly, or do any long division when you're like this. Your whole system is primed for just two things: fight or flight.

When you are in the mood for seduction, persuasion or writing poetry, your body doesn't need very much oxygen. Chest breathing is necessary when you want to increase the amount of oxygen in your system, to quench thirsty running and face-punching muscles. When 'at rest', your body actually works quite hard to retain carbon dioxide (CO_2) in the lungs because it needs CO_2 in quantities far greater than it is found in the outside air. Along with respiration, one of the most important roles of the lungs is to maintain a healthy pH balance in your blood. Blood pH is maintained by keeping some CO_2 in the lungs.

When we breathe with our chest through our mouth, the body exchanges gas less efficiently, and the large passage of the mouth sheds CO_2. As the blood's pH changes, the blood vessels constrict, which limits the amount of blood that can get to the brain. The haemoglobin also develops a higher affinity with oxygen molecules, making the red cells more 'sticky', further limiting the amount of oxygen passing through the constricted blood vessels, like soggy flour in a sieve. Less blood gets to the brain, and releases less oxygen when it gets there.

Quite perversely, this means that breathing more causes less oxygen to reach the brain.

Lacking oxygen, the brain will signal to the lungs to breathe more, which in some people can lead to hyperventilation and panic attacks. Over breathing can be a major factor in asthma, and is linked with many respiratory, cardiovascular, stress and sleeping disorders. A permanently disturbed pH will cause damage to the entire body's soft tissues and cause digestive problems. The chest breathing muscles are in the chest and neck. They engage to lift your ribcage and shoulders towards your ears, lift your collarbone, and puff out your chest. Constantly using them to breathe will cause the muscles to cramp up, like your biceps do when you're carrying a load of shopping while waiting for someone else to find their damn keys. When we are continually tensing them to breathe, and our typing arms hang off them, these muscles don't get a chance to relax. This is why your neck and shoulders often feel like they 'carry' stress and form knots that require lovers or creepy bosses to massage them out. For some, the soreness and stress itself can become yet another source of stress. Physiologically, stress is one of the most amazingly self-perpetuating patterns we have.

So: chest and mouth breathing addles the brain, clogs the blood, disrupts the digestion and disturbs the sleep. It is bad.

Good breathing

- ✔ As you inhale, your shoulders and chest remain still.
- ✔ You draw air in through your nose.
- ✔ Air is drawn into your belly.
- ✔ You exhale through your nose.
- ✔ When you take a deep breath, your belly fills first, and then your shoulders raise up and your chest puffs out.

Speak for Yourself

✔ Your breaths are smooth and flowing between inhale and exhale, like a sine curve with a brief pause when your lungs are empty, and again when they are full.

✔ In these moments of pause, your breath is not locked by closing the airways.

✔ Your breathing is almost soundless.

✔ The texture of the incoming air is noticeable in how cool it is on the tip of your nostrils, but quite warm and moist feeling by the time it hits your throat (thanks to mucous and nose hairs warming, wetting, filtering and slowing the air as you inhale).

Why is it good?

The primary muscles of respiration are the ones you want to be using. They bathe in oxygenated blood while they work, so they never knot. They maintain a healthy CO_2 balance in your lungs, adequately oxygenating your brain. Using these muscles will calm you, and give you access to more useful thoughts.

The primary muscle of inspiration is your diaphragm, which is a fascinating, dome-shaped muscle that is attached to itself in the middle by a sheet-like tendon. It sits inside your ribcage, under your lungs, separating the lungs and heart in your upper chest from your intestines, liver and other 'guts' in your abdomen. When it flexes, the diaphragm flattens out and descends, drawing down on the lungs like a syringe plunger dropping, pulling in air from the outside. As this air is drawn in through your nose, the constricted passage slows the air causing your diaphragm to 'work for it', and encouraging better gas exchange in the lungs. The nostrils also wet, warm and filter the air, making it gentler on your lungs. The descending diaphragm then pushes down against your guts, causing them to spill forward slightly, also pushing against your back muscles and pelvic floor. (The pubococcygeus or PC muscle forms the floor of the pelvic cavity and stretches like a hammock from the pubic bone to the bottom of the spine.)

Once you've fully inhaled, the gorgeous criss-cross of your stomach muscles push back against the guts, working with your back and PC muscle, pushing the diaphragm up, expelling the used air back out of the lungs and through the nose. The back-pressure from the narrow passage of the nose will work against this, toning your stomach, and retaining some CO_2. The healthy, pH balanced blood will then pass freely to the brain, giving you access to all your clever thoughts and happy ideas. As the diaphragm glides over the oesophagus and aorta, it massages them, further improving blood flow and digestion.

This is healthy breathing. When you breathe from here you'll feel calm, and when you speak from here you'll sound compelling.

Do this:

Feel the difference between chest and stomach breathing

→ Think about an approaching deadline or looming problem in your life.

→ Open your mouth and breathe from your chest through your mouth, taking deep breaths.

You will probably start to feel a bit stressed and panicky – and stars will begin to dance at the edges of your vision. If you keep breathing like this, you'll get light-headed and further panic will set in as your brain is deprived of oxygen. Perhaps you're like me and the skin on your hands will also start to prickle. You're about to give yourself a panic attack, and all from breathing through your chest.

Now try the following exercises instead and notice how they calm you down.

→ Sit up or stand up straight.

→ Close your mouth and breathe long, slow breaths.

→ Exhale even slower than you inhale.

→ Draw the air down, deep, so it feels as if it's filling your stomach rather than your chest.

→ Focus your attention on how you feel, and notice your heart rate change.

→ Consider that same issue or challenge in your life.

You should notice that your thoughts now move more readily to find solutions, rather than dwelling on problems. Your physiology of calm has quite a remarkable effect upon your thoughts and decision-making processes.

Speak for Yourself

Take a long, slow breath, through your nose and into your belly. Do it right now. Breathe less than you'd like to, exhale slowly, and you will feel your system slow down. Let your eyes blink, slowly. Feel your heart rate slow. Allow your body to relax and let your mind think. Being able to calm yourself down is an invaluable skill, not only for your own mental state, but for affecting the mental state of others. Think about the people you like to listen to, agree with, and follow.

When you breathe from here, you will feel calm and speak in a commanding way. The voice that comes from your diaphragm carries weight, and carries far. People like to be told what to do by someone they admire, and they will typically admire people who are calm and can tell them what to do. The first step to commanding and persuading other people is to command your own body, so that your centred, stable state becomes an anchor for them.

After millions of breaths that are almost totally unconscious, it will take some time to find your diaphragm, and even longer to train yourself to habitually use it. I found mine in a rather strange way. Being an irksome little attention-seeker, I would search for ways to amuse people, so I made up the following game.

Do this:
Locate your belly breathing muscles

I call this exercise 'Pregnant, not pregnant' and it's pretty simple.

→ Standing up 'nice and tall', suck your guts in, up into your chest cavity so that your stomach pretty much disappears (it may even go concave). You should look very, very skinny around your waist.

→ Drop down your guts and push them out as far as possible. Accompany the pushing out by announcing 'Pregnant!' in a funny voice.

→ As you draw your guts in and up again, say 'Not pregnant' in another voice. It's great fun. I used a gremlin voice and have struggled to find one that's any funnier.

As your guts fell forward during that exercise you should have been able to feel that it was your diaphragm that was pushing them out. The next exercise is excellent for calming and centring your thoughts – to take control of your body and consciousness. You can repeat this as often as you'd like, whenever you want to feel calm. This exercise comes from an ancient Indian form of meditation called Pranayama (meaning 'life force'). It is perfect to use before a big meeting, job interview, public speaking engagement or even a date. It will calm you down and centre you, allowing you to order your thoughts and imagine pleasing outcomes. While you breathe, focus on your desired outcome: 'I want them to feel relaxed', 'I want them to see me as capable' or 'I want them to end up nude in my bedroom' (depending on the situation, of course).

Do this:

Retrain your breathing

This exercise will help you find your diaphragm and use it to breathe. Here, repetition is key because you have a lot of un-training to do to remind your body of its biological baseline. The following will show you how babies breathe.

→ Lie on the floor.

→ Put a weight on your belly button. It can be a bag of sugar, a shoe, a book or a small child you don't like very much.

→ Lift the weight as you inhale.

→ Practise this again and again, always breathing through your nose.

→ Practise slowing down your breathing, and breathing longer, slower, and more controlled (and relaxed) exhales.

→ If your attention wanders, shelve the thought and refocus your mind on your breathing and the movement of the weight on your belly.

→ Make the movement smooth and even.

→ Allow a pause (without locking your airway closed) between inhale and exhale, and again between exhale and inhale.

→ Aim to make the path of the weight as smooth and steady as possible.

→ Continue for as long and repeat as often as you'd like.

As you do this exercise, try to focus on your breathing for as long as you can manage.

You should find that doing this activity will calm you down considerably. Your heart rate will slow, your mind will clear, and your eyes will blink slowly.

The purpose of these exercises is to help you to locate your diaphragm by exaggerating its movements. Normal stomach breathing is barely noticeable to other people when you're clothed. Moreover, stomach breathing will actually tone your stomach all day long. You'll get a flatter, sexier stomach if you use it when you breathe.

The controls for breathing are stored deep within the brain stem in our reptilian brain, owing to the evolutionary age of our lungs. The newer, fancier, more social bits of the brain are built upon older ones, and are further from the stem, mostly within the frontal lobe, the newest evolutionary addition. If you try altering your heart rate, you'll find that you can't, except by degrees, *through* altering your breathing. It is, in many ways, the deepest function of your body over which you have any conscious control.

Benefits of nose breathing

→ It slows the intake of air to make the diaphragm 'work' for it, making it stronger.

→ Nose hairs filter out that stuff floating in the air you sometimes see dancing in beams of sunlight.

→ The nasal mucous wets incoming air, making it gentler on the lungs.

→ The smaller passageway of the nostril slows incoming air; further filtering, wetting and warming it for the lungs.

→ It slows outgoing air creating back-pressure, and maintaining a healthy balance of CO_2.

→ It slows outgoing air to make the stomach work harder, toning your abs.

→ It encourages the calming parasympathetic nervous system response.

→ The restricted passage acts as a bronchodilator, meaning the lungs will expand and work better, giving you higher peak-performance.

→ It clears the nose of mucous blockages: *breathing through the nose actually makes it easier to breathe through the nose, as the incoming air pulls away mucous and expands the airways*.

The parasympathetic nervous system helps to calm the body, slowing the heart rate, lowering blood pressure, conserving energy and aiding digestion.

Benefits of stomach breathing

→ It encourages a calming parasympathetic nervous system response.

→ There is more efficient gaseous exchange, running your brain and muscles on better blood.

→ It maintains CO_2 in the lungs, thus maintaining a healthy pH.

→ Healthy pH means vascular and soft tissues stay supple and smooth with good blood resulting in better circulation, respiration, digestion and cognitive abilities – or breathing, eating, shitting and thinking as I like to call it.

→ Blood permeates the blood-brain barrier more easily, allowing you to think properly.

→ Using your stomach muscles helps tone them.

→ The stomach, lower back, diaphragm and PC muscles are all aerobic, meaning they need oxygen to work. These muscles don't hold and lock tension in, unlike the shoulders, neck and upper back which knot up and tire more easily.

You will need to remind your body to belly breathe for quite a while because you've got to re-wire years and years of repetition. The more often you can lie down and let your body experience the relaxing effects of stomach/nose breathing, the quicker it will unconsciously link the two and start doing it automatically. When you get stressed, remind yourself to breathe 'low, slow and through the nose'. You can get a similar effect by leaning back in your chair, crossing your arms over your belly and using them as a weight, lifting them as you inhale. The added weight will also help exercise your diaphragm as it has to work against the weight of your arms.

Speak from your gut

Having brilliant ideas is only useful if people get to hear them. We all hate that feeling of saying something interesting or funny and not being heard, only for someone else to say the same thing and get all the recognition. You must share your ideas so they can be heard, and heard in a way that they are believed.

It may seem strange to ask 'where' your voice comes from because most would say 'my voice box'. While that may be where the vibrations emanate from, the larger question is: to where do you let that resonate? A guitar's vibrations come from its strings as they're plucked, but it is the resonant chamber in the body of the guitar that gives it the sound. Smaller chambers will make the note higher and shallower, as with violins or ukeleles. When you breathe with your belly and speak from your diaphragm, you allow your voice to resonate down into your belly, making the sound rich and clear, like a cello. The sound need not necessarily be deeper, but rather it sounds richer, projects further and has much more vocal range.

Do this:

Where does my voice come from?

Before getting on to how you 'should' speak, it's useful to realise where you speak from now.

Use one hand to pinch (with two fingers and a thumb) either side of the bridge of your nose, and make a 'Haaaaaa' sound.

Make the 'Haaaaaa' sound come from your nose – you'll sound quite nasal and annoying. You should feel your nose vibrate with the sound as you use your tongue to fill most of your mouth, forcing the reverberations to bounce around in your nose (it might even feel tingly as if you're going to sneeze).

Use your other hand to touch your fingertips lightly against your throat. You want to feel all the vibration within the nose and virtually none from the throat. Steer the sound around within your head until you feel your nose vibrating wildly. You'll notice this is a very shallow sound with a very small area to resonate within.

Now make the sound come from your throat. Keep your hands where they are and you'll find it's a slightly richer, but still quite restricted sound. If you swapped your a's for i's, it sounds quite Australian.

Now move it to your chest: put your fingertips together in a point and press them to your breastplate. Focus on drawing the sound from your chest. Adopt a ▶

deeper tone if this helps. You should feel your ribcage start to vibrate gently with the sound, and not your throat or nose.

Now, having found what each of these places sound and feel like, speak as you normally would. Notice where the sound comes from.

I don't want to get qualitative and prescriptive, but I will. The further down you access your voice from, the better it will sound. At the very least, you want that range – you need to *be able* to speak from deep down in the gut. It doesn't need to be a deeper sound (though making one can help you 'find' it), but come from a deeper place. I say this often because people often think I'm training everyone to sound like Barry White. Though he sounded sexy, I don't think I'd fancy a woman who spoke like that.

Do this:

Get sound to come from your belly

Train your belly muscles to put power into your speech. You'll sound, and feel, much calmer when you speak. Your voice will carry, and people will hear all the delightful things you've got to say. To find and train these muscles, you must make silly sounds in private that nobody wants to hear.

With one hand on your stomach around your belly button, put the other hand on your breastplate. Start saying 'Haaaaaaaaaaa' from your chest as before. Now work on feeling those exhale muscles (your entire stomach) engage. The sound will gradually start to feel smoother and richer, and less gravelly around the edges. It may at first sound breathy and feel strange because you may have never used these muscles but be patient, this is not a 'bingo, I found it' exercise.

For the next exercise place one hand on your stomach and make a 'Psssshhhht' or a 'Ha' or 'Huah' sound. Feel your stomach muscles convulse to expel the air. This is where you want to practise talking from. Continue making 'Ha ha ha' sounds, allowing the stomach muscles to pulse with each exertion and expulsion of breath, going from full to empty in a pulsating motion.

Yes, that is a rather ridiculous exercise. I encourage you to keep making it more ridiculous (changing the 'Ha ha ha' to a French 'Aw haw haw' for example) to make yourself laugh. You'll notice that when you really do laugh, it comes from your guts. It's automatic, and it's happy. This is where your body breathes when it's happy and relaxed. This subtle difference between chest and stomach is what you're noticing when you think 'That's fake laughter' because it comes from the chest and sounds shallower, less hearty, and more deliberate. That's why we don't trust giggles because they speak of nervousness or desire for acceptance rather than real amusement. We really trust a good gut laugh, and very much enjoy causing them.

Where you're currently speaking from is fine, whether that be your nose, throat, chest or stomach. It is a pattern you have developed, partly through biology, partly through imitating your parents, through older kids you looked up to, and with your peers to fit in. Some of it also came from influences in your environment, from being a smoker or a sloucher, or from having to shout a lot. There is no 'right' way to speak and it's likely that you've learned a way that is very, very useful *for certain situations*. The wider the variety of situations you'd like to command, the more ways you'll need to be able to speak. Speaking well is simply a matter of having variety and being mindful of these previously automatic choices – and that what we're going to do.

It's up to you to experiment with different behaviours, notice how they feel, and see what works for you.

Just as diaphragmatic breathing makes you feel calm, speaking from your diaphragm and drawing your voice from your belly will calm others when you talk to them. When you speak from your gut in a mellifluous and captivating way, people will fall into what I call 'flow' with you, and they'll follow you, laugh at what you say and like you more. As you speak from a place that feels calm for you, they will feel calm. They will be drawn to that calmness because calm people have better ideas.

Do this:

Speak from the gut

Place one hand on your stomach and use the other hand to check that you aren't resonating in your throat, chest or nose by alternating it between them. Practise extending the 'Ha' to an 'Haaaaa'; and then a 'Hello!'

▶

This is a journey of self-discovery in its truest sense. Experiment with how many different ways you can do it, and remain aware of how each one sounds to you, and how they feel to say.

Extend the sound and feel what happens.

Keep extending the sound you can make with a long, controlled contraction of your stomach muscles: 'Hello, I'm bloody awesome and everybody fancies me' or something equally ludicrously, wonderfully positive. Owning this voice is about owning this mental state, holding it and sharing it.

It can take some work to learn to speak from your diaphragm. Give yourself time to find it and check how you're doing it (particularly easy to do while you're on the phone).

Pay attention to how you feel *when you're doing this exercise*. Don't get frustrated or chastise yourself if you can't get it right away, instead allow yourself to get excited when you are belly breathing or speaking from the gut. Notice and reward those moments, and notice what happens to the people listening to you. This mindful awareness (of dipping in and out of it) and positive reinforcement will equip you with a steadily increasing self-awareness and level of control over your breathing and speaking habits.

You will find that this voice will be similar to 'you' but distinctly different in a few ways. Your voice will carry further, and people will listen more intently. It's too much to expect to start speaking like this all the time, so for now just hold it within you and whip it out at certain opportune moments; perhaps when you need a large, noisy room to pay attention to your plans, or someone is in imminent danger and you need to talk directly to their reptilian brain.

Projecting your voice

Chest speakers allow the passive collapse of the chest to propel their voice. The flow of air is poorly controlled, so to increase volume, the chest speaker must nastily vibrate their vocal chords, causing them to wear and build up with scar tissue over time. You can hear this throaty gruffness in a regular shouter's voice. When they need to get a lot of force behind their shouting, some will hunch forward with the effort to expel air, and some will resort to shouting collections of two or three words per breath. When people shout they sound panicked, angry, and they seem as if they aren't really in control of themselves (remember at school when newly graduated or supply teachers would lose it and start shouting?).

When you speak from your gut, the stomach, your back and pelvic floor muscles engage to expel the air with exactly as much force as you choose. If you need to increase volume, the muscles engage smoothly and push out more air, while your voice stays calm and even. The voice has a larger chamber to resonate within, so sound waves bounce down deeper into the chest cavity, making the voice richer.

Do this:
Test drive your voice

Find a large empty space and test the full limits of your voice. You want to see how loud, deep, high, empathetic, certain, cowboy or Southern damsel you can sound.

→ Stand within the space and have a go at filling it with sound. Shout, and then try booming.

→ Say silly things, recite poetry, or read out the ingredients of a packet of muesli, it doesn't matter – you just want to feel how it sounds. You want to notice the effect that your own voice has on you.

→ Next, adopt 'character' voices. Imitate your dad and your mum talking. Imitate a school teacher, boss or workmate.

→ Put on the voice of someone you really admire. Get them to say the things they say to you, and say them exactly as that person says them. Hear their voice in your head and match the intonation, pace, volume and pitch.

→ Now speak as yourself but play with it until it comes from the belly and feels good. Notice how you sound as you bounce off the walls. Play with as many voices that could comprise 'you'. Make it loud and commanding, colourful and fun.

Let each progressive, different voice of you get louder. Really start belting the sound out. Really make some noise.

When you speak from your gut, the voice will go directly to people's subconscious. Famous biologist Richard Dawkins suggested that our response to these voices may come from our childhood, as we have evolved to listen to voices which are deeper than ours. Margaret Thatcher famously sought training from the Royal National Theatre to change her voice. Once you've mastered it, and have practised speaking from your diaphragm but maintaining a comfortable tone that feels natural, experiment with giving commands in this voice. If you are audible, clear and authoritative, people start to respond and obey before they've even really thought about what you've said.

Do this:

Put on your phone voice

When you're next making a phone call, focus on speaking from your gut. You'll experience what it's like to speak like this, and will be able to start introducing it into your face to face interactions.

→ Stand upright, put your hand on your stomach and feel it tense to push out the words in a controlled manner.

→ Let yourself relax and get into it – it shouldn't feel 'forced'.

→ Access the sound from your gut, it sounds richer, more melodious, but not that different from how you normally do. (If you start getting huffy or speaking deeply rather than accessing the sound from deep within you, the other person is likely to get weirded out).

The purpose here is to find that sweet spot where it just feels right, but different (too often we mistake normal for 'right'). Stomach speaking should sound only slightly different to how you normally speak – just a little bit more resonant and strong. Use this voice when trying to persuade people of something, when making a sales call, negotiating, or asking someone on a date.

Exercise to strengthen your voice

As you develop control and awareness of your diaphragm and stomach, you may also want to exercise the muscles of respiration. A weak core will make for a weak voice. Sit-ups can be good, but should always be balanced with back exercises (such as lying face down on the floor and lifting your face, shoulders and knees off the ground, or doing deadlifts at the gym). Twisting exercises such as cable crossovers will develop your obliques, and many can be found on the internet. Better than repetitive, limited movements are ones that fully exercise the range of your body, like dancing, capoeira or yoga. These will make your muscles fitter, flexible and more evenly strengthened.

The pelvic floor or PC muscle is very important too, for a variety of reasons. Firstly, it acts as the bottom of the abdominal 'box' – holding in your guts to stop them popping out your bum. Having a weak PC muscle will be like having a soggy-bottomed cardboard box, and you'll occasionally see some weightlifters who haven't trained their PC prolapse out of it under the pressure. The better trained your PC muscle (along with your back, stomach and diaphragm), the better your voice will sound. Secondly, and far more motivating: a well-toned PC muscle will dramatically improve your sex life. It will improve a woman's ability to orgasm, and allow a man to control his.

Checking in: breathing to and speaking from your diaphragm

So, how are you doing with all that? It's a lot to digest but the gist is fairly simple: breathe to your belly when you want to feel calm, speak from your gut when you want to exude calm. You should find that there are moments cropping up during the day when you have an opportunity to use them. Do so. These techniques are particularly useful at times when you might ordinarily get angry or upset because the breath, the pause, and calm explanation that follows (through a smiling mouth really helps too), will often totally change the focus of the discussion.

When you are about to have an important meeting or speak to a group of people, or do any important speaking, remind yourself of the previous exercises. If you can, find a private room and find your diaphragm and push out your voice. It will mean that when you give your talk, you won't have to focus on speaking from there but will be doing it, even if just a little bit, quite naturally. During the meeting or speech, occasionally pause and check in with yourself to make sure you're doing it, particularly when you deliver the most important part of your message in a clear instruction: 'Approve this project.'

Most importantly, remain aware of the effect your voice, and even your breathing, has upon others. Seek out feedback. You might even tell a friend or workmate that you're reading this book and get them to tell you what differences they're noticing (though be sure to get someone who is on your side – some people won't want workmates to outshine them, and those who neglect their own development will resent the development of others). Treat each of these exercises as experiments, and gather data on their effects. You should constantly be finding new voices that work for you and have the effect you desire. The art of trying out new things and reading the effects is more useful to you than any single exercise within this book. It's how I found them!

Using mindfulness to change your voice

Chapter Two

Bringing a conscious awareness to your unconscious behaviours is one of the most powerful things you can do with your brain. There are some amazing neurological findings that suggest even 10 minutes a day of mindfulness will improve cognitive function, reduce stress, and delay the onset of dementia. Whether it's for changing how you breathe, speak, or in the next exercises, how you stand and hold yourself, mindfulness is a way of tapping into your automatic behaviour, becoming aware of it, and altering it. The exercises on breathing have already introduced you to some of these ideas, as did 'setting yourself a reminder' to try out vocal techniques in social settings.

As creatures of habit, we tend to store processes that are familiar to us deeper in our mind. The more familiar they are, the better we get at them, and the further they recede from our conscious reach. Like tapping out a password we've used for a while, certain actions, and even streams of thought, can become pretty automatic. The process of developing these well practised habits is explained by Hebbian Theory, which describes how the brain grows and learns. It's neatly simplified in the phrase 'Neurons that fire together, wire together'. Donald Hebb theorised that through repetition, neurons that are used in repeated tasks clump together and develop strong, thick, rapid neural pathways. It's as if the electrical signals in your brain were cars. The more frequently travelled a route is, the larger, smoother and faster the road – from small tracks up to super-highways. Hebbian Theory explains our ability to develop a 'muscle memory' for certain tasks, like tying our shoelaces. Unless we've learned a rhyme, we struggle to describe the action of tying with words, and to do so we may resort to actually getting our hands to perform that beautiful 'loop, loop the loop, stuff it through' action (I actually had to stop writing and tie my laces to write that sentence). The more these stimulus-response patterns are practised, the stronger they get. Mindfulness is the ability to consciously access and alter these automatic functions.

Taking time to focus on our patterns allows us to deliberately build pathways to more productive, self-aware behaviour.

There are many, many books on mindfulness and its relationship with breathing. I won't go into too much detail here other than to simply mention the practice because you'll be using this idea of exercising deliberate control over largely automatic behaviours in many (if not almost every) exercise in this book.

Do this:

Mindfully breathe for ten minutes

I challenge you to do this exercise because it's one of the most difficult things you may do in this whole book. Lie down and concentrate on your breathing for 10 minutes. Two minutes seems like an hour. Your mind wanders. That's fine, let it, but bring it back and keep breathing. Keep directing your mind to focus on your breathing and notice the difference within your body. Let your awareness rest on every part, your skin, the texture of the air, your heart beating. You may even notice it beats more slowly on the exhale, particularly if you exhale slowly. Do this for a whole 10 minutes. If you want to have a fat and fit brain when you're 80, do this exercise once every day for the rest of your life.

Build new habits with mindfulness reminders

I would like to share with you the most useful tools for altering our habitual behaviour. I used it when I was wandering around a park at night with some friends as a kid. We met two older teenagers and started chatting to them. The slightly more drunk one said to me 'You have a really terrible posture, man.' I was shocked and quite upset. I realised that if he only said that because he was drunk, everyone else must be thinking it and not saying anything. So I decided to change the way I stood. The challenge with permanently changing how we breathe, speak, or noticing what we do when we're socialising is that we are so rarely aware of it. We don't make 'decisions' but act on autopilot, just as I never 'decided' to hunch my back. As a tall person, stooping to fit into conversations had become automatic. I was so shocked by this kid's harsh (but important) feedback, I wrote a 'P' for 'posture' on the back of my left hand every day. Every time I saw it, I'd check how I was sitting or standing and adjust my posture. After doing it 20 or so times every day, I started noticing that I already was sitting upright and soon a slightly more reasonable posture was my new 'normal'.

That is what we'll call a 'continual' reminder. You can set them to remind yourself to breathe well, speak well, and become more mindful of your physical presence.

Remind yourself:

→ to rewire yourself to breathe low, slow and through the nose;

→ to adjust your posture;

→ to speak from the diaphragm;

→ to be aware of enunciation, projection, inflection, pace or pause;

→ to spot social dynamics that may normally pass unnoticed (taking stock of where people are sitting, what kind of energy is in the room);

→ to cleverly lead a conversation or group of people towards more enjoyable topics of discussion.

As reminders you can use:

→ a letter or symbol drawn boldly onto the back of your non-dominant hand;

→ Post-it™ notes around the house (hidden inside the bathroom cabinet, for example);

→ Post-it™ notes in your drawer at work;

→ a phone reminder that will ping you at random (or pre-programmed) intervals;

→ a phone app that will do it for you.

Pirate reminders: AAR! (Aware, Adjust, Reward)

No, not Blackbeard! Here are some handy reminders I put together myself.

> **Aware** Ask yourself: 'How am I sitting/breathing/whatever, currently?' and 'Was I aware of this before I was reminded?'
> **Adjust** your behaviour. Let it settle in, and hold it for a while.
> **Reward** yourself (even more if you were already doing it).

Ways to get the most out of reminders

→ Make it clear: a very short word, letter or symbol works best.

→ Make it positive: a reminder to 'not slouch' will be less effective because if you are slouching when you see it, you'll get cranky at yourself, and if you aren't slouching, you'll feel nothing. If your reminder is to 'sit up', then you'll feel good when you're doing it, and be focused on your goal.

→ You must act, even if it's inconvenient, every time you see the reminder (otherwise it becomes a source of disappointment and hence annoyance).

→ Choose a place or form of reminder that occurs enough times to make a difference. Ideally, you want to find that sometimes when reminded, you're already automatically doing it.

→ Reward yourself: it can be as simple as noticing the difference in how you've been feeling as a result of this change. Enjoy the experience. Tell yourself you're fabulous for taking control of your existence. Smile. You can even allow yourself indulgences, so long as they are in line with your goal.

Do this:

Create a continual reminder

Using the tips given, create a reminder to change a habit. Focus on doing something, rather than not doing something (standing up straight, rather than 'not slouching' for example). Set the reminders and use them to change your behaviour.

Contextual reminders

Perhaps you want a reminder for something that happens only in certain contexts, rather than all the time. Think about someone with whom you have a recurrent disagreement or friction, perhaps your partner, a family member, or someone at work who you've known for a long time. Think about what fires it up, and what you do, say and think in response.

Tell yourself that next time you're in that situation, you'll remember to stop and AAR!, and alter this pattern. By doing things differently, you'll give yourself more choices. With 'aware' you're not just becoming aware of what's happening, but you'll be aware of *what you want from this situation*. What you want should be broad and positive, 'winning' an argument is not a useful outcome. Having the other person feel better about themselves is a useful outcome.

With that scenario and others that I've used, I've been endeavouring to paint vague pictures of examples that are universal, in the hope they paint vivid pictures in your mind. My hope is that when you read them you're reminded of something happening in your own life and will think: 'I just read about that!' and will then remember to AAR! to give yourself more choices. That is how you set contextual reminders – create a vivid imaginary scenario and be ready to spot it when it happens. You can set a reminder to AAR! anytime you're frustrated or upset. When the reminders occur to you, pause and become aware for a moment. As you breathe, centre yourself and ask 'What do I want from this interaction?' then try something different. You don't necessarily need to 'fix' patterns, just adjust them continually until you get a pleasing outcome. Absorb that pleasing outcome as your reward. Or give yourself some chocolate.

Another way to reward yourself is the practice of gratitude.

Do this:
Practise gratitude

Being grateful for what you have has a profound and measurable effect upon your mental state. Practise this now, and take time (particularly when you're feeling down) to revisit it. Write out a list of things for which you are grateful. Be as expansive and specific as you can, from the bare necessities of 'I have a home' (if you have one), to detailed things, like friends, lovers or particular skills your life has afforded you the opportunity to learn.

Mindfulness reminders will be particularly useful in the next section, in which I'll be encouraging you to change the way you stand and physically interact with the world around you.

Create a captivating storyteller's voice

Chapter Three

Most people don't think much about *how* they speak until they think they're doing it 'wrong', and then they often resign themselves to accepting it: 'Yeah, I mumble a bit, I know.' Thankfully you, dear reader, are mindful, self-aware, and capable of taking responsibility for how you're being received. You are willing, nay, *eager* to adjust how you speak, and to try new things that may at first seem strange or out of character. As you go through the following exercises, you will realise that tiny changes to your speaking will seem huge to you, while remaining barely noticeable to anyone else.

There is a remarkable thing that happens in the mind when it hears word spoken in a certain way. And I don't mean in a 'certain' way like it's an unknown entity, I mean spoken with certainty. Have you ever been told something and immediately believed it to be true? Most of us have experienced this, while other people tell us things that *are* true and we instantly doubt them. Clearly spoken words make ideas sound clever.

With a rich, mellifluous voice colouring your speech, you can experiment with ways to captivate your listeners. Later in this book we will look at some techniques to draw people into what I call 'flow', which is a trance-like state of fascination with someone. Part of that fascination comes from how you use your voice to flesh out the meaning and emotion of each idea, exercising the full range of volume, pitch and texture of your voice. Over the following pages, you'll develop your storyteller's style to develop clear enunciation and simplicity of speech; and the crafty use of inflection, modulation, pace and pause.

Take a moment to think about three compelling speakers. Go online if you can and find some videos of them speaking, and take note of how they speak. As we cover inflection, modulation, enunciation, pace and pause, notice how they use each of these elements when they speak. My favourite speaker is George Carlin, a comedian who died not so long ago. He paints pictures with words and infuses his stand-up routines with poetry, rhythm and rhyme, and relates strange ideas in a multitude of different voices. When I listen to him I feel as if I'm being drawn into a whirlpool of amusing and confronting ideas, and the world around me disappears. Steve Jobs was also an impressive orator and I'm sure there are some other excellent storytellers who are not yet dead. Find some of your own, and as we go through the next section, adjust your style using elements of each of the speakers as a reference.

Speak for Yourself

The basic gist: you'll need to focus on using downward inflections at the end of statements, modulating your voice, slowing your speech, and saying more with fewer words.

Inflection

The way we inflect our sentences has a significant affect on how we (and the things we say) are received. Downward inflections at the end of sentences make them sound like statements or instructions. Upward inflections sound like questions and invitations. Upward inflections invite critical evaluation. Both can be useful when used mindfully, but when we're not aware of what we're doing, our inflection can sometimes undermine our message, and other people's faith in our ability.

Many Western English speakers have a habit of asking questions instead of making demands or statements. It has its benefits, in that it allows for degrees of urgency. We have everything from 'Would you mind?' all the way through to 'I'm serious, do it' to indicate levels of severity. When you read the last two statements just now, it's likely the first had an upward inflection and the second a downward one.

Making demands as if they're questions, like 'May I have the bill please?' has some disadvantages. It takes longer to get the bill, for starters. Certain people, and certain cultures, add an upward inflection to the ends of their sentences as if everything is a question. It's called the 'high rising terminal' (why it is both 'high' and 'rising' I do not know). Even when some people are telling someone their name, it sounds as if they are meekly asking for approval: 'I'm Joe Bloggs?'

Try it. Introduce yourself out loud, as if you're meeting someone important for the first time. Notice how you inflect your voice. Try it with an upward inflection and then a downward one. Notice how it feels to say each one, and how they sound.

Upward inflections invite critical evaluation

An upward inflection can turn a statement into a question. Indeed in French, it is often the only thing that signifies a question: 'Go to the train station' with an upward inflection becomes 'Are you going to the train station?'

An upward inflection also indicates that someone has paused in the middle of a thought: 'She went to the station... to buy a ticket to Paris.' The effect can be useful to draw people in, as following the upward inflection we are inclined to ask ourselves 'Why did she go to the station?'

Become aware of upward inflections in your own speech and you can use them quite craftily. If someone makes a statement and you doubt their honesty, simply repeat their exact statement back to them with a subtle upward inflection: 'You sent the brief on Monday (?)'

Downward inflections indicate certainty

A downward inflection instructs others to believe and to obey. It's no coincidence that newsreaders, priests and politicians tend to use downward inflections. These are statements of authority. If you've ever heard someone say something so confidently and matter-of-factly that you've immediately believed them, then this is how they were speaking. Look at the time now and say it out aloud. Most people will tell the time with a downward inflection. Think of whatever news programme you watch, and say its opening phrase: 'I'm Indira Naidu, and this is the Six O'clock News.' The downward inflection will be on 'o'clock news'.

Do this:
Test your inflection

Read the following statements and questions out aloud. Record them and play them back to yourself. If you don't have a voice recorder in your mobile phone, there are always plenty of free apps.

Relax and speak the following statements as you ordinarily would. Don't read it as you speak it. Read the sentence first and then say it aloud after you've read it. This will encourage you to speak with your normal inflection.

Statements and questions
→ I am learning how to inflect my voice differently.
→ Have you ever paid attention to your inflection?
→ My name is [your name].

▶

Speak for Yourself

→ I am [your name].

→ I am very perceptive.

→ Would you give me your phone number?

→ You're fascinating. Give me your phone number.

→ I think we should schedule a meeting for Tuesday because it comes after Monday.

→ I am perfect for this job.

→ I think I'm pretty organised.

→ It was a pleasure to meet you, I'll see you tomorrow.

→ That is very interesting, I'm going to try it.

→ You are quite perceptive.

Listen to the recording. Notice how you are using inflection.

Record the statements again. Make a 'Pssshhhht' sound, find your diaphragm and speak from there. Inflect each point 'properly' (use downward inflections for statements and upward inflections for questions). With the sentences in two parts, try inflecting up in the middle, down at the end, and then try both with a downward inflection.

Go back through the list and inflect your voice 'improperly'. Use upward inflections for statements (making them sound like questions), and downward inflections for questions (making them sound like statements). With the two-part sentences, inflect down in the middle and up at the end (that will feel very strange).

What you may notice while doing that exercise is that upward inflections, even when used 'improperly', have their place. If you want to get everyone to share their ideas and opinions, perhaps on a creative matter or something as simple as 'Let's go to the pub (?)', upward inflections on statements let other people feel that their opinion is valued, and they are more likely to offer it. If you're meeting people for the first time, there's often value in sounding inclusive and reasonable, rather than authoritative and certain. Build your awareness, and you'll soon find certain circumstances when inflecting your voice differently will yield remarkable results.

The fastest method to develop the practice of using inflection mindfully is to edit your own speech in real time. When you say something and can hear the 'wrong' inflection (when I say wrong, I mean ineffective rather than incorrect), repeat the statement immediately. This mindful practice in a social setting will work to quickly rewire your inflection habits.

Modulation

Modulation is that undulation in tone that turns words into music and can hint at the mood of what you're saying. It's different from inflection, but quite similar. Modulation adds feeling, while inflection adds meaning. Modulating your voice well monopolises the attention of your listeners, ensuring that they feel the emotions of a story and are spurred to action.

Husky sounds are great for something heartfelt like 'You are really very important to me', or for saying something conspiratorial as it can sound like a stage whisper. Matter-of-fact tones are for sharing information, while jokes often have a 'Weey-heey!' sort of sound to suggest a punchline (particularly if the joke is quite cheesy). We know most of these so naturally, using them is simply a matter of letting yourself.

Use a storyteller's modulation to colour your words and add emotion or meaning. It will fascinate your audience and keep them hooked to what you're saying. Be bold with it because if you're someone who doesn't usually do it at all, you'll need to push it to extreme lengths before anyone else even notices – such is the way our brains are wired.

Enunciation

What we say is not important, it's what's understood that matters. The more clearly you speak, the clearer your thoughts will seem when they reach the mind of your listener. If you mumble through words, they'll be difficult to understand, and they'll come across as garbled and incoherent. Your ideas – your precious ideas (!) – will seem unimportant and confused. When you speak words clearly, snap each word apart, polish them up and present them nicely; people who hear those ideas attach a similar sense of value and clarity. You'll notice this when you decide whether to follow instructions. A large part of that decision will rest upon how clear those instructions are. If we know what we're doing and why we're doing it, we're much more likely to comply.

The larger the room, the noisier the setting, the more foreign the audience or the further they are from you, the clearer you'll need to be. Open your mouth and speak more clearly. We never (or rarely) think 'That person speaks too clearly', but we often hear people and think 'They mumble'. If you're going to err on any side, go for clarity.

Do this:
Limber up your speaking bits

Follow these steps to stretch and exercise all of your enunciation muscles before you give a presentation or do something important (it can even help before dates or when networking as we don't much enjoy talking to people if we continually have to ask them 'What?').

→ Scrunch your face into itself, push your eyebrows together, wrinkle your nose, and squash your mouth together and towards your nose while making a 'smushing' noise. Then open your face, lift your eyebrows, open your eyes and open your mouth as wide as it will go.

→ Shake your head from side to side, letting your cheeks slap against your teeth while making a 'Uuhhhh' sound. Let your lips go as floppy as they can.

→ Blow a raspberry with your lips and tongue. Go from a tighter mouth and higher pitch to floppy lips and more exaggerated flapping. Make the vibrations so strong that they tickle your lips. There should be spit on this page.

These exercises may do more than limber up your speaking muscles and allow you to enunciate more clearly. There's evidence to suggest they will increase the secretion of elastin, delaying the onset (or slowing the growth) of wrinkles. So you'll sound clear and look good, too!

Do this:

Tongue twisters

Practise doing tongue twisters before you speak, and you'll speak more clearly. That way, you'll sound confident and your ideas will seem clever.

Repeat the following words, speaking as clearly as you can, and really using your whole face, mouth and tongue to shape the words very ob-vee-us-leee:

→ red leather, yellow leather;

→ unique, New York;

→ the lips, the teeth, the tip of the tongue, the tip of the tongue, the teeth, the lips;

→ red lorry, yellow lorry;

→ she sells sea shells by the sea shore;

→ Peter Piper picked a peck of pickled peppers; A peck of pickled peppers Peter Piper picked.

Whenever you're speaking and someone says 'What?', that's feedback. They can't understand you. You're not making yourself understood. We all have a limit to how many times we'll ask someone to repeat themselves. For some, that limit is zero. If one person asks you to repeat yourself, there are probably two or three others who resigned themselves to guessing at what you're saying; or just laughed politely, and hoped like hell you were trying to be funny.

The moment someone asks you to repeat yourself, increase your volume significantly, slow your speech dramatically, and enunciate every syll-a-ble clear-ly. We do a lot of our listening with our eyes, watching the shape that the mouth is making will change how we hear the sound. The more you open your mouth and exaggerate its movements, the more easily you'll be understood, obeyed and liked.

Do this:
Enunciate a story

Get a story book or a magazine article and practise saying words aloud as slowly and clearly as you possibly can. Put on a storyteller's style and really get into it. Make your whole mouth move to shape each word. Don't let k's and t's drop off the end of words and don't let collections of words run together – snap them apart, polish them up, and clearly punch out every sound.

Try to defy your native accent. If you're Australian, try saying 'wa-ter' rather than 'wau-dah', and if you're English say 'hat' (with a huffy aitch) rather than 'at'. If you're American, stop saying 'aloo-min-um' altogether. It's alu-*mini*-um.

Pace and pause

Great speakers have an ability to draw their listeners in as much as through what they say as what is left unsaid. Practise using pauses to slow your speech. Pauses let people ponder. The more we feel that we're being left to decide something ourselves (rather than being yammered at and harangued into agreeing), the more likely we are to consider the idea favourably.

'We often speak quickly when we think 'This is boring, so I'll say it quickly' or we get nervous and our heart rate and adrenaline increases our physical processes. It's quite common that we listen to people and think 'Woah, they speak *way, way* too fast' but quite rare that we think 'They talk way too slowly.' Slow down. Modulate your voice. Pause, and let people think. If you really care about what you're saying and you're certain you're right, then pause.

Say fewer words

When you do the following exercise on slowing down, you'll notice that a lot of the things we say are empty words. We end up 'filling pauses' with 'Um's and 'Ah's. We let our minds catch up while blathering out meaninglessness such as 'It's like…' and 'Y'know' and 'It's sorta'. One of my favourites is 'So what we're gonna do, is, we're gonna...'. Chop it all off – it just serves to make the message more confusing. Repetition is bad because you may be thinking 'I wasn't clear about this', but your listener is often thinking 'Does this person think I'm an idiot?'

As you slow your speech, you can enunciate each word more clearly and choose each word deliberately. As you learn to say more with fewer words, your messages will become more memorable and infinitely easier to listen to.

Do this:
Transcribe an explanation

Get a voice recorder, and call someone up for a chat. Include an explanation of how to do something, or a story of something that happened recently. It must be brief, and consist of only 30 seconds to one minute of speaking.

→ Record only your side of the conversation.

→ Listen back to it, and write out a word-for-word transcript of what you said.

→ Get a red pen.

→ Put a line through all the place holders, such as 'like', 'sorta' and 'y'know'.

→ Put a red line through 'filled pauses' (words like 'um' and 'ah').

→ Put a red line through any time you repeat yourself.

→ Put a red line through anything that is obvious through other things you've said.

→ Put red lines through any needless information, e.g. 'It was her cousin's father's friend's dog' and when the specifics of the relationship are not important to the listener's comprehension.

→ Put a red line through anything else you consider to be unneccesary.

→ Take a look at all the red lines.

Go back to the story or explanation. Think about the current level of understanding of your listener and corral all the information you'll need. Order your thoughts, hit record, and say it again, simply, clearly, *slowly*, and using as few words as possible. Listen to yourself and get a feeling for how much more better you sound when you say less.

Whenever you're asked to talk about something (particularly if you're explaining something or trying to persuade someone), take a moment to summon all the relevant information to mind *before you start talking*. Take a breath (to the diaphragm, obviously), order your thoughts and then speak. Your first word should not be 'Um' or 'So...'

Set yourself reminders to slow down and see how slow you can possibly get before people start to tune out or freak out. Start including the things you've experimented with such as enunciation, inflection and modulation, and try them out in social or professional settings. You'll be struck by little 'Aha!' light bulb moments, and once you make it work for yourself, you'll become more likely to deploy these techniques naturally in your everyday speech.

Do this:
Play with the storyteller's style

Write a speech on an issue that you care about. Include a mixture of statements and rhetorical questions. It should be something heartfelt, about yourself, or something that is very important to you. Practise saying it out loud a few times, mixing between upward and downward inflection.

Modulate your speech as much as you can, use pauses after important points, and speak slowly and clearly. Practise speaking from your diaphragm, and infuse what you're saying with passion. Make it sound like a call to arms, like William Wallace's 'You may take our lives...' speech from *Braveheart*.

When you've got it, record it and play it back to yourself.

Write down how you sound, focusing *only on the positives*, and use first person language, e.g. 'I sound like a leader' or 'I sound like I know what I'm talking about.'

Physical confidence

Chapter Four

Confidence is a strange word. When you feel good about who you are, and eager to engage with new people and share your ideas, we call that confidence, and with that feeling comes power. It changes who you are, at your very core. It radiates through your behaviour and into the behaviour of others. The challenge with the word 'confidence' is that it's spoken as if it's an emotion, like happiness, or a personality trait or innate characteristic that some have, and others don't. It's not.

A philosopher and polymath from the 11th century called Avicenna created a thought experiment called 'the floating man'. He asked us to consider a man suspended in the vacuum of space, unable to see or hear anything, arms and legs splayed so that he could not feel anything, even the sensation of himself; and then to consider the form of this man's mind. Avicenna's idea is supposed by some to have been a question of the existence of the soul, and today lets us ask questions about what it means to be self-aware. My gut feeling is that without having an 'other' to perceive, and without anything at all to perceive, and a language to perceive it within, the floating man would probably have a brain that resembled a raisin, and a mind that was awash with formless emotions and something like ideas, but ones which would exist beyond our comprehension. This thought experiment also raises the question: does our physical form shape our thoughts and feelings, or is it the other way around?

Do I stand up and speak out *because* I'm confident, or am I confident *because* I do that?

'Confidence' is not a quality you can use. Confidence is not an emotion. It is a feeling of assuredness, and it is contextual. I would feel very confident if you asked me to twirl a flaming bow staff because I'm good at it and I've done it many times. I would most certainly lack confidence if you asked me to land a jumbo jet because I've never done that and would probably kill everyone on board. Confidence comes from experience.

You will not become confident by chanting pleasing mantras at yourself.

You will not become confident at meeting new people by reading a book.

You will not become confident at public speaking by avoiding it 'until you're ready'.

You will only ever get confident at things by doing them, not the other way around.

Speak for Yourself

I studied theatre at university and played many different kinds of characters, from brash, loud-mouthed louts, to shy guys and detestable man-whores. The directors of these pieces of theatre would have me build each character from the ground up. We would get the basic information about the character from the lines of the play, and I would then have to imagine the character's upbringing, their desires and fears. Using a slightly hypnotic technique, we would explore, mentally and physically, how that character fitted within my body. I would become aware of which part of my foot touched the ground first when I walked as that character, how my arms hung at my sides or swung as I walked, and how I walked over rough terrain or dealt with a difficult-to-open jar. Through the posture and shape of my body, the character would have a natural response to other people, and fit within a social hierarchy. If you stand tall, look people in the eye, speak clearly, calmly, and command people with downward inflections, you are the boss. This is true of monkeys, humans and dogs, too. You don't 'pretend': when you stand and move in a certain way, you think and feel a certain way, and it becomes natural.

What became fascinating was how the experience of being this character would stick with me. After the curtains closed, the applause died, and the dishonest praise subsided, I would find that elements of that character had become a part of me. I played a nerd on the bus in some invisible theatre (which is acting in public, in such a way that the audience weren't aware they were watching an act). Days and weeks after playing the nerd on the bus, I continued to feel quite shy, and other people would treat me as such. They would stand next to me while I sat, and I noticed how I'd feel uncomfortable and small as they looked down at me, patting my shoulder and tilting their head at me while they spoke. They saw me as shy. I saw me as shy. A while later, I played an incorrigible womaniser in a musical. With a swagger and a devilish grin, I exuded self-assuredness that was repulsive to watch but great fun to play. While first developing the character, I was not very good at holding eye contact, but after time, the urge to break eye contact waned. I started to behave as if my eye contact was a gift, to them, one that they'd enjoy. And they did. And I started to believe it. It was quite enjoyable – a lot more enjoyable than being the nerd on the bus. From my many experiences of stage personas bleeding into my ordinary life, I developed a fascination with behaviour that led me to seek out research that would prove my suspicions were founded in fact.

The science of standing tall

If you're ever part of a behavioural study, you can be pretty sure that you're being lied to by a psychology professor. Richard Petty is one such liar. He once told participants that they were testing a brand of headphones to see how well they stuck to your head. Thankfully, most participants in behavioural studies are university students, and their excessive alcohol consumption often renders them incapable of asking questions like 'Why is a psychology professor doing research on headphones?' The participants in Richard's study were divided into groups. One group was asked to swivel their heads from side to side (to imitate shaking the head as if to say 'No'), while the others moved their heads forwards and backwards (nodding as if to say 'Yes'). While the participants nodded and shook, they listened to an editorial from the campus radio suggesting that students should be required to carry identification cards. The students' head shaking and nodding measurably affected how strongly they were to agree with the broadcast*. None of the participants were aware that the nodding or shaking was influencing their opinion. Richard also did research that asked participants to either sit up straight or slouch while writing their personal qualities which would be relevant to attaining a specified job. Sitting up straight caused students to have greater confidence in what they'd written, while slouching had the opposite effect on their peers. Our physical form influences our perception of ourselves, even without our conscious awareness (and perhaps partly *because* we lack that awareness). It runs counter to the common assertion of shy people who think 'I'll stand up, speak up, and look people in the eye when I'm confident and have that job/car/house/partner.'

When Avicenna was writing about the floating man, he was proposing a dangerous thought experiment by asking people to question whether the soul was part of the human body or distinct from it. It was revolutionary. In our modern age, the prevailing philosophy has persisted with a notion of dualism, considering the mind and body to be different, one in the other, but not *of* the other. Our bodies seem

---

* Though in a quite particular way. Instead of being more or less likely to agree with the story itself, the nodding students were likely to be more certain about their own opinion on the issue.

to be meaty, ungainly and functional, while the mind is a masterpiece and has separated us from monkeys and turtles. This concept of dualism is so seductive, it persists even today. When people talk about 'mind and body' they are still succumbing (at least colloquially) to the idea. What Richard and many others in his field are suggesting is that our bodies are fundamentally part of our experience of the world, and that our posture and physical form strongly affect how we feel and what we think. This kind of research on embodied cognition suggests that the link is so fundamental, we often aren't even aware of where our ideas finish and our physical behaviour starts. We are making discoveries that have broken the divide between mind and body, and I think we are on the precipice of breaking another boundary – between self and other.

Power poses

Amy Cuddy has done some amazing and highly publicised work on 'power poses'. It is very exciting but has been covered extensively, so I'll rush through the details here and get into the 'how we can use this' stuff as quickly as possible. Amy asked participants to wait in a room while holding either a high power pose (sitting with an arm across another chair and legs splayed; or feet up on a desk, arms folded behind the head) versus a low power pose (sitting hunched, legs together, head bowed) for two minutes. She took mouth swabs before and after, and found that some very interesting things happened. Holding a high power pose resulted in an increase in testosterone (which signals dominance, yes, even in women), and a decrease in cortisol (which is a stress hormone). Conversely, holding a low power pose resulted in a drop in testosterone and an increase in cortisol. The poses were altering the participants' chemistry and quite fundamentally changing their experience, making them feel the emotional qualities that those poses embody.

After posing for two minutes, the high power posers felt more confident and less stressed. When given an opportunity to gamble, they did so, much more than those who'd been sat in a low power pose. Participants were then asked to meet and talk with a panel of judges who were unaware of the participants' posing. The testosterone-pumped, high power posers were rated as more likeable and capable than their cortisol-infused counterparts. Changing your posture, even for two minutes, can change how you feel, behave, and how others perceive you. Our physicality offers an opening through which we can change how we feel about ourselves, and through that, change how others feel about us. By adjusting our physical presence, we can kick-start a socially enforced, self-affirming cycle of confidence. This is very exciting stuff.

Faking it?

Amy Cuddy did some amazing research and gave a wonderful talk at TED (Technology, Entertainment, Design). It was beautifully spoken, had an intensely personal element of vulnerability, and it shared some groundbreaking science. Even so, I bristled when she used the phrase 'Fake it till you make it'. I worry that the concept of 'faking' it is an unhelpful idea. When you sit or stand upright, when you draw your shoulders back, open your eyes and smile, when you walk and talk and interact with the world purposefully, in a way that feels powerful, you will feel the happiness and confidence and all the emotions that go with these physical states. Your body will react, your chemistry will shift, your mind will change. Others will see that, and their thoughts about you will change, the way they respond to you will also change. That is not fake. At most, it's unfamiliar. These behaviours may not be a part of your day to day patterns or a part of your usual posture so it feels different.

Different is not fake.

Amy warns that you maybe shouldn't put your feet up on the desk during a job interview, and suggests doing power poses in private. My worry is that doing these things in private may diminish their power, particularly if you feel the need to revert to your 'true' self when you're around other people. Doing static poses, briefly and in private, may cause the chemical boost to wane over time as they start to become a symbol (to yourself), but lack the social validation that comes from the confidence feedback loop of being seen standing tall.

Find ways to replicate Amy's amazing results, in public, in motion, in a way that feels authentic. Do it constantly, in extremes in private and in small but significant and socially acceptable ways when you're in public. Experiment with what form your body can hold that will elicit that sparkly-eyed attention from others, and you'll rapidly start to believe in your own confidence. It will feel different at first, but soon it will normalise and become a part of your behaviour. You'll live on a confident, stress-free high, while still being fundamentally you.

With regard to Amy's 'fake it till you make it' statement, there are social constraints and dynamics of certain friendships that can seem to be violated if someone 'changes' who they are. Drastic changes to social dynamics can be difficult, and we must be honest and accept that shy people's friends like them, in part, *because* they are shy. There is something dark in each of us that doesn't like to see other people being happy. We all benchmark ourselves – it's unfortunate, but that doesn't mean we should pretend it isn't there. So, if the idea of being 'fake' works for you, then go ahead and use it, just ignore this part and read on.

So...

Sit up straight. Open your eyes. Smile. Act as if you're confident, happy and alert and you will be. In time (about two minutes) you'll start to feel better. At first the effects may feel minuscule, and your brain will find logical ways to explain them. Stick with it, using continual or contextual reminders. Ask yourself: how would I be if I always breathed through my diaphragm? How would I be if I always spoke clearly, stood tall, looked people in the eye and smiled? Hour by hour, day by day, your life will start to change. You might not be aware of it, but what is the value of awareness when you're more happy, confident and successful?

From power poses to a power presence

Many of us have an idea of 'good' posture being stiff, bolt upright, and 'correct'. It's not. A good posture is fluid. It radiates agility, grace, fertility, flexibility, control and confidence. A good posture moves. Sometimes you might saunter like a cat, sometimes prowl like a lion. A good posture should be able to pick a pen from the floor without groaning, and straighten again without propping itself up on a table. A good posture can glide between pedestrians on a busy pavement. It should be able to get into and out of chairs without using its hands. A good posture should not be a posture at all, but a fluid way of being. It is a presence.

Amy's poses had to be static and predefined, so her results could be measured and replicated by others. You are not doing science, you don't need to be measured and replicated. You're doing life. Instead of posing in private, I'd like you to build a whole physicality that stays with you. It is you choosing a physicality that represents yourself however you choose. It is permanent and fluid, adapting to each situation just as we adjust our breathing when we enter the water.

The following exercise asks you to examine the qualities within you that you most want to accentuate, and to pretend that they're controlled by dials. You will experiment with dialling each up and down to find a sweet spot that feels good and gets you what you want. This is the same technique that actors use to build characters, but here, you're building an ideal physical version of you. Do it first in private to see how it feels, testing each dial at its extreme; and then experiment with bringing them out in public. You'll find that you already have these qualities within you (courage, humour, intelligence, perceptiveness, an air of competence or whatever you choose), in differing intensities, and in certain contexts. This exercise encourages you to bring the physicality of those moments where you exhibit the quality into new contexts – at job interviews, meeting a room full of strangers, public speaking, negotiating, or asking for a raise.

Do this:
Define your key qualities

Decide on some qualities you'd like to embody. They can be confidence, calmness, competence, curiosity, and that's just the C's. The easiest way to do this is to write out a long list, and choose three that don't overlap and are meaningful to you.

Write about times in your life when you have demonstrated that quality. It's certain that you will have. If you can name it, you have it, you simply need to turn it up. Let your mind tick back and find one of those moments.

▶

Describe what happened, how you felt, what you did and what the result was. It should be relatively short, and filled with emotive and multi-sensory descriptions of sights, sounds, smells, textures, feelings and thoughts. Once you've written it, tell the story aloud using everything you've learned about speaking from the gut, inflection, modulation, pace and pause. Notice how it feels speaking like this, about these qualities of yours.

If you want to embody 'confidence', you must decide what that is. For most, it's having solid eye contact, standing tall, being open, keen to meet new people, happy to crack a joke, and laughing loudly. These are qualities you can build into your character. You will need to do the same for qualities such as being capable, kind or calm. The next exercise will get you to turn this idea into a character, and your character into a caricature that is beyond lifelike proportions. Take it to the extreme and you will experience a lingering sense of energy, excitement or positivity. The awakening of those happy, confident neural pathways will make them more accessible to you during ordinary life. You will start to walk taller, taking slightly longer steps, looking people in the eye and smiling more often. It will naturally happen and reinforce itself because your whole being will enjoy doing it. The more you reinforce (by frequently doing character building sessions or accentuating the effects throughout the day with reminders), the stronger it will get.

Do this:

Build an ideal you

You will need: an empty house or office, somewhere you can be sure that you will not be seen or interrupted. It will need to be a large area with a lot of floor space for you to walk around, with a chair or sofa too.

Consider your first key quality. Hold it in your mind and with your breathing, encourage other thoughts to drift away on each exhale. You are meditating on one quality.

Allow yourself to notice where in your body you are feeling it. Check in with your body and notice how this feeling affects your hands, feet, eyes, legs, calves, ▶

elbows, stomach, chest, neck, head, the expression on your face and the sensation of your eyes. Imagine in your body where it is the strongest and focus on that.

Open your eyes. With full focus upon this quality, bring your awareness to your environment. See how you relate to the furniture in the room, the walls that surround you. Notice your own clothing and arms and legs.

Enjoy it for a moment.

Start to move. Notice how you stand, where the urge comes to move, how long your steps are. Experiment with everything, from whether your hips lead to how your feet hit the ground, to whether your shoulders roll while you walk. Continually change every part of your body until it fits with this quality you're holding.

When it fits, exaggerate it. Exaggerate it more, and more, and more, until you're walking (or perhaps moving) around in a totally bizarre way that is completely alien to you, but which represents this quality of yours, to you, physically. When it's at its peak, choose a gesture that will remind you of this state. Do that gesture while you're in this heightened state.

Dial it back down to a reasonable level, letting it simmer while you imagine how behaving like this would affect your life in the future. Imagine it vividly – see, hear and feel this version of you in meetings and presentations.

Drop it and shake it off. Then do the same for your next key quality.

Then, combine all three.

The next challenge is to bring your 'new' self into a social setting. The more often you do exercises like the one just given, and adjust them by changing the qualities you use or changing how they affect you, you'll find that they will start naturally seeping into your everyday life. Your body will think 'You know, I think I'd feel much more comfortable if I sat like *this*'. Social beings that we are, and with such a thin wall of skin between self and other, it can be hard (and at times inadvisable) to totally change how we are with others. I'm sure you'd feel a bit strange if your best friend suddenly started behaving quite differently. To work around this quirk, it can be good to work *with* this quirk. Conscript a friend or two and tell them what you're doing. If you go out one night or are about to go into an important meeting, tell them 'I'm trying something new'. It will bring them on side, as discussing it will make it a part of your social contract with them, making them feel good about helping you change.

It can also be useful to 'test' this new behaviour in environments which are new to you. Holidays can be great for that because they already encourage it (when, but on holiday, do we shriek and laugh and take photos with strangers?). New workplaces and meetings with people we don't know can also be a good testing ground to try things out, notice how it feels, and the differences in how people respond to us.

Do this:
Test out your power presence

Notice when you're next in a situation that calls for one of these qualities (perhaps a disagreement, a negotiation or meeting, perhaps you want to catch someone's attention or put on a swimming costume and jump in the pool).

Give yourself permission to behave differently and repeat the gesture that reminds you of the physical presence of that quality. Change your shape, embody those qualities. Really let your imagination amp it up, so when you do the gesture you feel a surge of energy that you struggle to contain.

Restrain the quality, and the physicality, ideas and feelings behind it. You don't want to let too much out. Hold it in, imagining it to be so strong that some still seeps out. Enjoy it. Perhaps you stand taller and look people in the eye and speak more clearly. Perhaps you laugh more.

How are you going with all that?

So, let's recap on things so far.

→ Breathe to your belly, speak from your gut. You'll feel calm, and when you speak from there, the sound of your voice will calm others.

→ With downward inflections, you sound authoritative.

→ With musical modulation, you capture the attention of your listeners. Your pace and pause will let them listen, while they think for themselves.

→ Practise clearly and deliberately enunciating your words – you'll find the thoughts they speak will be clearer.

→ Thinking more about how you walk and move, and sit and stand differently will, moment by moment, alter your chemistry and change your whole outlook on life.

How's it all going? It is quite a lot to take in, and you won't fall into doing these things instantly. It'd be a little bit disappointing if it were that easy, wouldn't it? No? Perhaps not.

One of the primary things you may have found yourself working against in the first part of this book may have been yourself – your own feeling of 'this isn't me'. That's okay, it's natural, but don't succumb to it. Allow yourself to try these things on, like a fancy jacket, and see how it works for you, not to 'change who you are', but to give yourself access to new ways of being. Seek to make it work for you, and as different elements of each of these exercises fade from your memory, come back to them and try them again, until they feel natural, and together they can become a part of a new 'you'.

The Words

Part Two

The presence you've worked on developing in The Voice will be invaluable here. Feeling that you're in that 'character' will allow you to relax and speak more comfortably, and this section will give you a script around which you may work. Some of the techniques will at times feel like you're working hard against yourself, to 'stop' doing certain things and focus on doing others that might seem abnormal. As much as you can, focus on *letting* yourself, rather than *making* yourself. Once you've experienced the effects of many of these techniques, you'll find yourself using them more often, and as you build a repertoire of experience, it will start to feel like a habit. You'll probably recognise that you already did some of this stuff anyway, in certain situations. You'll have a commanding presence and be persuasive and engaging, while the final part, The Style, will focus on breaking all the rules and putting yourself back into what you're doing in a courageous and distinctly humorous way.

In this section, you'll learn the following things.

→ About 'flow' – a mental state of singular focus and a trance-like entrainment between people. Discover how to spot it, enter it, and entice others into flow with you.

→ How to listen to people's words to discover their motivations.

→ We'll discuss persuasion techniques, including hypnotic language and a variety of biases.

→ How to listen to your words, and the effect your words have (on you and others).

→ How to use their own wording to speak to people 'in their language'.

→ How to combine these techniques to persuade others to do stuff with you, for you or to you.

Go with the flow

Chapter Five

There exists a thoroughly studied and poorly understood mental state that has fascinated humans for hundreds of years. It has been explored by meditating yogis and Zen archers, potters, poets, performers and long-distance runners; even data-entry clerks have experienced this state. It is a state of total focus and it's been called a great many things, and here we'll call it flow.

It's likely that you dip in and out of flow many times every day, when you knit or do filing or jog on a treadmill. Depending on how well I'm writing, you may even be experiencing it now. It's possible that if you were in flow, my drawing your attention to it has pushed you out of that state and into a state of half-reading and half-thinking, about your thinking, or something other than the words on this page. It's a slippery sucker. Flow has been described in a multitude of different ways, as a trance, as being in 'the zone' or 'zoning out', of getting in a 'groove', or getting 'lost' in a particularly engaging activity or story. If you've ever driven or walked somewhere, and arrived at your destination as if on autopilot, unable to remember the journey, you've experienced it (that particular phenomenon is called highway hypnosis). It's a state of immersion, where your intense focus upon a single task causes the world around you to fade from your awareness.

A rather amazing individual with a very confusing name coined the term 'flow' to describe this state. Mihaly Csikszentmihalyi conducted some fascinating research which discovered an interesting relationship between our ability to focus and how that affects our enjoyment of life. Mihaly had participants carry pagers which would ping them at random intervals throughout the day to ask them three questions: 'What are you doing?', 'What are you thinking about?' and 'How happy are you?' His results made for very interesting reading: those who were more focused upon whatever they were doing, *regardless of what they were doing*, were far happier than those who were daydreaming, multitasking, or focused on something other than what they were doing.

The answer is to 'monotask'. Focus on what you're doing and you'll get better at it. You'll be happier as a person too. You'll also become more successful at it, and more happy about *that*. Once you become adept at inducing and recognising this state (or *experiencing* it), I will encourage you to speak in a captivating way that induces these states of flow in others. When you read it and experience it again, you'll probably think 'Oh yeah, I've done that!' and it's probable you have. I'll just be encouraging you to do it mindfully.

Speak for Yourself

Do this:
Experience flow by drawing circles

Get a note pad and pen, and start drawing circles, going around and around, over and over again, focusing on the task of drawing perfect circles. Occasionally stop, change the page, and start again. Keep going at it and notice that quite often you're best at it when you're not thinking but just 'doing'.

It's important to find what induces states of flow in you, and practise that. Active pursuits like riding a bike, playing an instrument or practising a skill are more effective because they give you something to focus on and learn (whereas meditation is great at inducing a state of flow, but trying to focus upon nothing makes the state quite difficult to maintain).

Do this:
Find another activity that induces flow

Get into an activity with which you are familiar. It should have some level of challenge (Mihaly points out that flow occurs best when your level of ability is matched by the challenge of the task), and preferably be repetitive or at least rhythmic. If you don't have such an activity, get one! It's good for you. Try learning to juggle, knit or play an instrument.

Engage in this activity for a while and let yourself get into a state of flow. Dip in and out of awareness of your mental state and develop a conscious awareness of it, going back to experience it as you focus on what you're doing. Do this for at least 10 minutes every day. If you do this activity for a living, all the better (not actually that crazy as you can focus on doing even menial tasks more and more efficiently until the demand on your mind pushes you into flow).

In flow with others

As social creatures, we sometimes fall into trance-like states of entrainment with one another, which I see as another example of flow. Inducing flow states in others is simply a matter of monopolising someone's attention – quite literally captivating them. When someone mumbles, fidgets and self-deflates their own ideas, listeners can easily absorb all of the information they're outputting while still entertaining private thoughts like 'Aww, they seem nervous' or 'I wonder who's playing at the bar this weekend?' When you look people in the eye and connect with them; are expressive, emotive and enunciate clearly, using your face, arms and whole body to create immersive ideas and vivid images, you become a raging torrent of information. Reading and interpreting all that data will monopolise the listener's attention and draw them into flow, along with the thoughts and feelings you're expressing. This is how we get excited by listening to an excited speaker or saddened by listening to a particularly painful story. Vivid imagery, good stories, rich emotions, metaphors and immersive imaginings are powerful flow inducers. So is speaking simply and passionately. Experiment with it. Watch for changes in your audience, continually alter your style and tinker with how you present your message until they sit there, wide-eyed, stock-still, and focused intently on you.

When people are in flow, they breathe, blink and drink in time with one another, and fall into step with each other when they walk. They think the same thoughts, feel the same feelings, and start caring about each other's welfare. Chanting, clapping and singing together will cause people to fall into flow with one another, which is why churches and cults favour that behaviour over rational discussions.

I should mention at this point that this kind of 'flow' is being used in a slightly different way to that which Mihaly coined. His focus was more upon the engagement in solitary activities to find flow, though he does mention it is something that can happen between friends. I'm using flow because there are so many other terms people use that I don't quite like, such as being in a 'trance' or a 'suggestive state' (which seem so devious), or 'mindful' which at times implies the opposite (to me it seems like there is no 'mind' in this process, just immersing yourself in the experience). NLP practitioners describe this connection as 'rapport', which is a word I like, but among that community the idea has taken on an almost supernatural meaning. Rapport to me, and in the way it is used colloquially, is different. Rapport is an *expectation* of flow. It's knowing that you'll be in flow with someone when you're with them. You can have rapport with your best friend when you're nowhere near them, just by knowing them, sharing the same values, and getting on with them well. Rapport is somehow removed from *what you're doing*, and is more about *who you are*. As such, I don't believe it's possible to have 'instant' rapport, while you can create an instant(*ish*) sort of flow with someone. We're using the word flow because 'flow' conjures up an image of direction and a sense of 'going with' it (which is exactly what we do), and it also has a variable intensity, from a trickle to a torrent.

Do this:

Have a conversation and get someone in flow

We're going to look at some techniques for getting people into flow in a little bit. For now I'd like you to go out and have a crack at it. I want you to do this because once there are ideas and theories to learn and apply, something that is natural to do can become confusing. I want you to be sure that you already can, and do, create flow with people.

So now, while you're capable of getting yourself into a mindful state, where you're aware of your body and are speaking from your diaphragm, have a chat with someone. Use your soporific voice and tell them a story (stories are particularly effective at inducing states of flow). Notice when your calm, controlled, comfortable (and comforting) physical state begins to affect them.

Easy methods to find your flow:

→ tell them a story;

→ talk to them about something that excites them;

→ make them laugh.

You know they're in flow when you spot the following.

→ Their facial expressions mimic yours.

→ They distractedly use the same word you used just a moment ago.

→ They drink, blink and breathe at the same time as you.

→ They hold their their breath momentarily when you stop talking.

→ Their eyes match yours: if you widen your eyes, theirs will widen too, and if you look at something, their eyes will follow.

→ They attempt to sustain or increase physical contact with you.

→ They attempt to sustain or decrease the distance between you.

Mirroring

Mirroring is a deeply ingrained evolutionary trait, which we exhibit automatically and subconsciously whenever we're in flow with someone. You may have noticed this kind of mirroring before, perhaps mimicking the posture of a boss, or saying something in time with a friend, or noticing a listener widening their eyes when a speaker expresses surprise. When you're mirroring, you're increasing your similarity to someone within that moment, and as a result, they'll like you more and become more inclined to agree with you, buy stuff from you, hire you or help you out. We like things that are like us – preferring family members over foreigners, and dogs more than frogs. Copying people's body language, posture, rate of speech, movement, choice of words, clothing or beliefs will make you more similar to them in that moment. They'll start to feel an inexplicable affinity with you. We've evolved the habit of mirroring because it helps us form and recognise the in-group, so we can bond with them and persecute the out-group more efficiently.

How to check if someone's mirroring you

→ **Legs** – we'll often fall into step with people as we walk.

→ **Body** – when people are in flow, they imitate one another's posture.

→ **Head** – when people are in flow, they tilt their heads to the same side.

→ **Pace** – some people can influence our state, speeding us up and getting them excited, or calming everyone down.

While you already mirror people naturally, there is a benefit in developing an awareness of what you're doing because there are times you might not want to mirror someone (when seeking to establish social dominance, perhaps, or when you don't want to get upset and drawn into a negative space), and times when you normally wouldn't mirror people in which perhaps you should (while talking to a shy person, if you want them to open up to you).

Mirroring people deliberately

You can also quite deliberately let yourself mirror people. I say 'let' yourself because I'd like you to focus on them, get into flow with them, then follow that automatic urge to mirror them. If you mirror people deliberately, it can become a little bit eerie, particularly if they notice you're doing it (which is likely because as you fall into flow and your thoughts become aligned, your awareness of your posture will make them aware of it too).

Mirror people in subtle ways that feel natural and comfortable to you.

→ Notice how they sit and mimic (rather than exactly copy) their posture.

→ Match large gestures with large gestures and small ones with small.

→ Match their pace. If they tap their feet, tap or jiggle something else at a similar pace and if they're slow, be slow too.

→ Speak at the same pace and volume.

→ Use the same words they use.

→ Match their inflection and modulation.

When we call it 'mirroring', there is a temptation to sit face to face with someone. If you can, avoid that and try to sit side by side. This will allow the other person to go off into their own space rather than being forced to focus on your presence in front of them. Remember, mirroring is a subtle art and people should not consciously notice that you're doing it.

Mirroring is particularly useful when you want:

→ to get people to see things from your point of view;

→ to feel the way they do, and see things from their point of view;

→ to wind down conflict, by mirroring them and letting them mirror you, then subtly leading then towards a relaxed state;

→ to fit in with new groups;

→ to negotiate with someone, getting them to want what you want.

Do this:

Mirror someone

This is particularly good in coffee shops, restaurants or places where people are sat down. It's difficult to chase someone while mirroring them.

Find someone you'd like to talk to (that you don't know already) and notice everything you can about them.

Start from the ground up and observe the following things.

→ How are their feet touching the ground/each other? (Are they crossed – and if so which leg over which – flat, bent or straight?). What position are their legs in?

→ Are they slouching, leaning forward, sitting upright, slightly twisted or leaning to one side?

→ Are their hands moving? How fast? And what are they doing?

→ Are they speaking, nodding, looking everywhere, looking at other people or avoiding attention?

Start copying their body language a bit at a time. You may notice that if you let yourself (and you like the look of this person), you will probably have started copying them already. Make some assumptions about their life.

Go and talk to them: say hello. Sit down and have a good old chat. If you are doing this well, they'll want to talk to you because something in their deep, herdlike brain is saying 'one of us' when they look at you. At the very least,

▶

pretend you think they've dropped something and say a couple of words. Test the assumptions you made about them (because guessing without testing is baloney), by casually asking them some probing questions.

Consider when you're talking to someone who's shy. You can see that they are avoiding eye contact, taking up less room, hunching and hiding from the world, and you think that they're shy. When you hunch and hide from the world and avoid making eye contact, as they are, you *feel* as they do. You'll have a much richer experience of what shy is *for them*. As Amy Cuddy demonstrated with her research, the body reacts chemically to this posture. Now when you think about new concepts or opportunities, you'll notice that they seem intimidating rather than exciting. When you feel like this, ideas about safety and security are much more appealing than ideas of 'challenge'. When you are mirroring them, you won't need to 'know' or 'think' that, you'll *feel* it.

Good speaking is mostly listening

Chapter Six

With all this stuff about speaking, it's important to mention the value of shutting up, of asking questions and listening. Listen to what people are saying and how they're saying it. Become genuinely fascinated by them. Ask them what they do (for enjoyment as well as for work), and you'll learn useful information about their circumstances, values, ideas and motivations. These are clues to building a solid friendship or working relationship, and this information is invaluable when it's time to persuade them of something. You'll also learn some interesting stuff about how cars work, clothes are designed, or the politics behind ping pong tournaments; and make a new friend in the process. We all see ourselves as interesting, and it feels lovely when other people recognise that.

A commonly espoused practice is that of 'active' listening, which we see practised by eager salesmen, psychotherapists and professional ladder-climbers. 'Yeah?' they'll nod, excitedly, 'Oh really? Wow!' and the nodding will increase until their heads look as if they might detach in a violent flurry of I'm-really-truly-listening oscillations. I'm not so sure about 'active listening' because people appear to get a little bit too excited at *seeming* like they're listening, which often comes across to the speaker. It also promotes paraphrasing. Paraphrasing is useful for testing to see if you actually have understood something, but that is only useful for double-checking instructions or technical concepts. Understanding another person's emotions is impossible. Emotions are felt as feelings but communicated as words, which for each of us will have slightly different connotations.

When I say listening, I mean authentically listening: actually be interested. It's not hard. Ask them questions, offer insights, and probe at things which interest you. Listen to the words they use, and when you do speak, use those same words. When you use their words they will really feel understood, and when they feel understood they will be happy to shut up and listen to you.

Copy their wording

We love the sound of our own words, probably more than we ought to. Think of how it feels when you meet someone and they express an opinion that you also hold, in exactly the same terms that you use. You will usually feel excited, validated and you'll immediately see that person as more intelligent (because you're intelligent, and that's why you think those things, right?). You'll like that person and be more inclined to agree with them on other issues.

Richard Wiseman mentions the effect of copying someone's wording in his thoroughly readable self-help book called *59 Seconds, Think a Little, Change a Lot*. He cites a study from a bloke called Rick van Baaren:

> '[They] descended on a small restaurant and asked a waitress to help them. After showing customers to their table, the waitress was asked to take their order in one of two ways. Half the time she was instructed to politely listen and generally be positive by using phrases such as "okay" and "coming right up". For the other half she was asked to repeat the order back to the customers. Repeating the order proved to have a remarkable effect on the tips the customers left.'

If you asked them, I doubt any of the diners would say 'I tipped her more because she repeated my order to me', but something about copying their wording made them feel like giving the waitress more money. Use the words that people use. When people refer to something as a 'project', don't call it a 'job'; if they say it's 'difficult', don't call it a 'challenge'. You'd think we all mean the same thing when we say these words but we don't. Talk in the same terms. The more closely matched your words are, the more closely matched your minds will seem.

Clean language

When we want to show someone we understand, there can be a temptation to pre-empt what they are thinking or feeling by saying things like 'You must be angry...' Doing this will pollute the conversation with your presuppositions and your dirty words. Instead of 'angry', they may have described their feeling as 'confused' or 'hurt'. They will now have to deal not just with their problem but with *your understanding of it* (and if what they are experiencing is negative, this can be particularly sensitive). Those are dirty words.

Instead, ask what are called 'clean' questions – an idea invented by a chap called David Gove. Clean language seeks to remove the asker's preconceptions from a discussion. Devoid of your assumptions, you get much more meaningful words, which represent, to the other person, a more pure idea of what they are experiencing. Hear these words, remember them, and insert them back into more questions. Remember the answers too. When it comes time to speak, use their words and your messages will be much, much more targeted to your listener.

Developing questions

'**What is it about that?**' or '**What is it about (X)?**' are clean questions which allow you to get down to the core of an issue. You can ask people 'What is it about *that*?' over and over, again and again. Each time you'll get down to a deeper issue or core value. Discussions that start off talking about money will often become an issue about power, freedom and travel or about getting stuff done before I die. When it comes time to speak, and you string these motivators together, your message will be far more persuasive than it would have been if it were phrased from your perspective.

All people make sense to themselves. If you can't understand why someone is acting in a certain way, ask questions.

Dirty questions

→ **Why did you do that?** This assumes there was an intent, when it could have been a mistake; and 'why' questions often evoke logical, rationalising, self-justifying answers.

→ **Are you upset?** This assumes an emotional response, and a negative one.

→ **Was that after you talked to X?** Trying to guess at something doesn't help. Just ask 'When was that?'.

Clean questions

In each of these, substitute the capital letters for whatever words they used.

→ Where is/was X?

→ That Y, what's that like?

→ Then what happened after Z?

→ Is there anything else about X?

→ When did Y happen?

→ What needs to happen for Z?

These questions are useful in a variety of situations. In the following examples, assume that the underlined words are ones which have been spoken by whoever you're talking to.

→ That recognition, what's that like?

→ Is there anything else about getting a pay rise?

→ What is the relationship between your boss and feeling valued?

→ When you have a car with good fuel efficiency, then what happens?

'...in what way?'

'...in what way?' is a particularly effective clean question because it can follow almost any statement, and for some reason it elegantly drills down to the core values or ideas that people hold dear. Perhaps it's effective because it can seem strange or weirdly worded. To almost any description of an emotion, event or causal chain, you can ask it. If someone says 'I feel overwhelmed', you can again ask them 'Overwhelmed... in what way?' and they'll often give you a metaphor or something visceral that you can really get stuck into. It will be a more emotive and useful answer than those evoked by 'Why?' questions, which receive less useful, more logical responses.

If you're going to ask a 'why' question, stop and ask 'In what way?' instead.

✗ **Don't get justifications or 'logic'** by asking 'What do you mean by that?' or 'Why is that?'

✔ **Do get more useful answers** by asking 'Excited, in what way?'

Search for the desired state

When you want to motivate people, ask questions which will lead towards solutions. You'll find that just asking such questions will often be enough to resolve an issue.

→ **What would it take for (X) to happen?** This assumes it would take something for X to happen, and assumes that X *can* happen.

→ **What would influence your decision on this?** This assumes something would influence their decision.

→ **How would you like to be seen?** This assumes they would like to be seen at all.

→ **What would X like to happen next?** This assumes X would like something to happen.

→ **How does X feel about that?** This assumes they feel a certain way about it and is useful if you want to establish that a certain behaviour should stop, when they have not yet accepted that they want it to stop.

→ **Is there anything else about that?**

Using exactly the same words someone just said may at first seem strange, but as you become practised at it, you'll notice people will start to feel that you just *get* them. The more you do it, the more natural it will feel, and you'll be able to do it while staying in a state of flow with them, rather than having to think about it. You will have a richer and more accurate sense of the whole situation, understanding the desires and motivators of the players within it. You will understand them better, and they'll be beset by a desire to get to know you. If you do need to understand things in your terms (perhaps their choice of word seemed out of context), you can say 'Exciting? What do you mean when you say that?' to get a fuller understanding – and even more words to parrot back at them.

Using clean language in...

Sales

Don't let your assumptions drive the conversation. Sometimes a car salesperson's intimate knowledge of a product will cause them to blather on about engine size and power to weight ratios when their customer might just want a nice colour. Find your customer's criteria for making a decision, and what each of those criteria mean to *them*.

If they want a <u>fuel efficient car</u>, you need to know what it is about <u>fuel efficiency</u> that's important. Perhaps they want to be seen as a good person, to <u>feel good</u> for being <u>environmentally friendly</u>, or perhaps they just don't want to spend much on fuel.

Drill down past 'fuel' by asking 'What is it about <u>fuel efficiency</u>'? to get at the underlying motivation.

They might say 'Caring about the environment is important to me.'

- ✘ **Don't say your bit:** 'Well the Prius has great fuel efficiency and looks a bit like a spaceship...'
- ✔ **Do use their words:** 'So what about <u>caring about the environment is important to you</u>?' then they'll say something dull and you say '<u>Helping future generations</u> in what way?'

Keep asking more questions until you hit their deeper, personal motivations. Remembering these motivators will allow you to use them to construct your pitch using exactly the same wording they did.

Managing people

When you lead people, most of what you're really managing is their emotional state. Particularly on matters of emotion, avoid offering suggestions. They'll usually sound glib or make the person feel misunderstood, and they don't want to see their upsetting circumstance as easily fixable. Use clean questions to find what they want, how they feel, and what gets them excited.

When people are upset, the most important thing is to make them feel understood.

- ✘ **Don't suggest:** 'If you just talk to her, I'm sure you can sort it out.'
- ✔ **Do ask questions:** 'And then what happened?' and '(X), what's that like?'

Let them explain how they feel. Provided you don't dwell on it, describing what we're experiencing is an important step to solving problems, because it lets people feel they 'got it off their chest' (which I think is where the value starts and finishes). Then use clean questions to get them moving towards a more positive mental state.

Use 'What's important about that?' questions to discover how they see themselves and what they want from life. Quite quickly you'll find that most people have rather huge goals and strong moral values – often even ones they've never really thought much about or ever talked openly about before. Knowing that someone wants to be a caring person, or seen as intelligent, or to 'make a difference in the world' is valuable for persuading them to speak up, work harder or, in some cases, quit and find a better suited job.

Do this:
Solve someone's problem by asking questions

Next time a friend or workmate complains to you of a problem they're experiencing, coach them with clean questions. If you feel the need, let them know that this is a 'technique' (to explain the departure from your normal behaviour), suggesting that it may help them to get a handle on their issue.

During this whole process, you're avoiding offering interpretations, input and advice. Be as <u>clean</u> as possible. It's actually quite difficult because we so often feel 'Oh I know what to do!' or 'I know what you mean' but that rarely helps.

→ Get to the core of the issue, how they feel and what everything within it 'means' to them. Continually use their wording within each new question, while keeping it casual and not too psychoanalyst-y.

→ Ask what they would like to have happen.

→ Ask them 'What would have to happen for X to happen?' and other questions about how their desired state might occur. Get them to pose all the solutions themselves, and make sure they devise more than two.

Pitching for or presenting your work

Much like the diners in the restaurant, your client or customer wants to know that you've heard what they've said exactly as they've said it. Ask them all the questions and summarise their desires at the end – not in your own words, but in theirs.

Remember those words, write them down if you must. When presenting your work back to the client, remind them what they said – 'As you said, John, you wanted it to <u>communicate energy</u>, and Karen, you wanted <u>bright colours</u>.' They'll feel as if they've already had an impact on the project and feel less like changing it arbitrarily once it's finished (which people often do, particularly with artistic endeavours, just to feel like they 'did' something. Note: a cunning way to deal with this habit can be to leave in a single, relatively obvious and easily fixable error in your work, which they will then flag and you can fix without going back to the drawing board).

- ✗ **Don't say 'Yeah, we get the gist':** 'Great, so that's all clear. We'll be back to you within a month.'

- ✔ **Do repeat their words exactly:** 'So to clarify, there are <u>three issues</u> you want this project to address. They are <u>efficiency</u>, <u>ease of use</u>, and as you said Gemma, <u>it should look sexy</u>.'

Dealing with conflict

Most conflict comes from a feeling of being misunderstood. Set about understanding who you're talking to.

Whenever you need to describe someone else's behaviour, strip it back and present it as cleanly as possible. Describe events and their results, but *do not* use emotionally laden or judgemental words like 'annoying' or 'disruptive'. Rarely does anyone describe themselves as 'disruptive', so they'll respond negatively to such interpretations. Don't paraphrase things they've said. Use words they'll recognise, descriptions of behaviour with which they must agree, and then describe the effect that behaviour has upon you or others. Be specific and speak in terms with which they cannot disagree.

- ✗ **Don't be general and negative:** 'You've been hostile lately and it's annoying me.'

- ✔ **Do give specific and non-judgemental examples:** 'When I said what I thought, you said "No" straight away. The same thing happened yesterday when I was talking about whale mating rituals. What's going on when that happens?' Listen to the answer and then tell them the effect: 'It makes me feel like what I'm saying doesn't matter to you.'

Do this:
Win an argument by turning it into a discussion

Next time you're in danger of getting into a disagreement with someone, do the following.

→ Assume that you don't understand them. Express that, kindly.

→ Get them to explain; both what is happening, and how they feel.

→ Repeat it back to them, using exactly their wording.

→ Get them to express their desired state.

→ Dig into what their desired state means for them.

→ Encourage them to propose <u>three</u> solutions.

→ Describe their solutions in your own words to see if you've understood (logistics require comprehension, emotions don't).

→ Ask how they will feel about that solution.

→ Repeat back to them how they now might solve it, and will feel about their solution.

→ For extra points, try to make them laugh the entire time (more on this approach later).

Speak for Yourself

The art of persuasion

Chapter Seven

That is probably the most exciting and scary heading in this whole book. We spend a large chunk of our time and brainpower trying to find ways to persuade people, so that they hire us, enjoy our company, agree with us, do things with us, to us or for us. Most of all, we want them to *want* to do these things.

Laying facts out as premises and conclusions in a logical order does have its place, but that place is quite small and overcrowded. Besides, facts are terrible motivators. If you want to change what someone thinks, offer them facts. If you want them to act, you must affect how they feel. Use clean questions to find out what they value, and why they value it. Naturally, you'll be using your voice and your presence, getting in flow with them, and letting them mirror you as you copy their wording when you speak.

Focus on what you want

This is important for persuasion and invaluable for life. Steve Jobs didn't make Apple computers by wanting to be 'less poor' and 'make fewer awful computers'. Lance Armstrong didn't take drugs and win seven Tour de France titles because he wanted to 'ride less slowly' or 'lose less often'. Anyone who's ridden a motorbike will tell you that a rider who focuses on 'not hitting potholes' will spend a lot of time clattering through potholes (a phenomenon known among bikers as 'target fixation' where focusing on what you want to avoid will draw you towards it). You will not become a beacon of popularity, persuasive and powerful by wanting to be 'less shy' or 'less awkward when meeting people for the first time'. These ideas don't motivate us to do something as much as fill us with a fear-fuelled energy to do *something*, without having a clue *what*.

Do this:
Write out your goals

Write out a list of reasons for reading this book. Add some more that are broad – in terms of what you want from life and why you want it. Do this now.

▶

Speak for Yourself

Next, underline any motivations for reading this book that are phrased in the negative, i.e.

→ 'I want to be less...'

→ 'I don't want...'

→ 'I felt/feel [negative emotion]'

→ '...don't want...'.

Underline any reference to an undesirable state, e.g.

→ poor;

→ lonely;

→ sad;

→ ignored, etc.

Rewrite the list with goals focusing towards what you do want. Anywhere where there are comparative or vague terms, remove them (so 'more persuasive' becomes 'persuasive' and 'quite popular' becomes 'popular').

Read over the two lists and notice the effect they have on you.

The same effects are in play when we're motivating others. Focus on what you want them to do. It is really important but often difficult to remember this. When we are close to a problem – perhaps a system at work that doesn't do what it's meant to do – we tend to focus on all the reasons that make it undesirable. When it's time to convince someone else that it needs to change, we spew out a long list of 'this sucks' and 'that's broke' and end up whinging at someone whose job it is to pretend to care. Consider what that's like to listen to. We might feel deeply unsatisfied with the current situation, but what then? Which of the multitude of other options do we take? The expensive one? The fast one? The difficult one? Complaints make the problem sound huge, and fixing the *whole* problem might seem too much to handle. Without motivation and small, do-able chunks, these kinds of discussions often end with 'Yes, we certainly should do something.' Then nothing gets done while people 'consider the options' but really just try to forget about it.

The list that is formed with a view towards your ideal state will give you a sense of determination and purpose. There's a focus. You know where you're heading. Some of the goals might seem daunting (in fact, if they don't, perhaps you should go back and scale them up a bit). If so, break them down into smaller, sequential tasks. When broken into smaller chunks, two things happen – the items all seem do-able, and an appreciation for how long it's going to take will often give you the kick you need to get going *now*. Notice this yourself, and focus on solutions when you talk with others.

Stop and ask yourself as often as you can: 'What do I want from this situation?'

- ✗ **Don't focus on problems:** 'If we don't do something soon, we'll be bankrupt by June.'
- ✔ **Do talk about what's exciting:** 'This is brilliant because we can cut costs while increasing profit...'
- ✔ **Do focus on the benefits:** 'It will make your work easier, giving you time to focus on the things that matter to you.'
- ✔ **Do focus on happy feelings:** 'It's such fun to use.'

The power of presupposition

We are highly responsive to other people's expectations of us. Presuppose that people will like you, and they will. Instead of 'trying' to impress them, you just let them be impressed. You'll be more relaxed and friendly, and as a result, more impressive. I don't mean to indulge in the hopeful delirium that imagining something will make it happen. It won't, but if you expect to encounter opposition, the way you choose and inflect your words, your body, the way you structure your message, and your interpretation of other people's words will all be skewed. When we expect resistance, we find it, and think 'I *knew* it!'.

Start with a presupposition that is helpful to your cause. Presuppose that people will see the value in what you're offering, be intrigued by your presence, or see the validity in what you're saying. It changes the whole tone of your message, down to your physical being. When people read a friendly, passionate or informative tone, they'll react with interest.

Experience the difference for yourself, right now. Recall one of those recent practice arguments you've had, you know, when you're driving or in the shower or washing up, and say your bit against your boss or partner or someone. Now, have that same one-sided argument, but this time instead of presupposing they will argue with you, presuppose that they'll agree if you present your ideas well enough. The difference will be huge.

Set reasonable, exciting and vivid presuppositions, and it'll start to feel as if they've already happened. These presuppositions, when vivid enough, will supplant the less helpful, self-destructive thoughts you might occasionally experience.

Persuasive presuppositions

→ Presume that your position is understandable, and challenge it to make sure it is.

→ If someone doesn't agree with you, it's because you haven't made yourself understood. Humans will agree unless they've heard different information or are motivated to disagree.

→ Before getting them to understand you, understand them.

→ Get fully inside their experience and expect that it will make sense once you are immersed within it.

→ Test it to see if they are right.

→ Presume that it must be right, *for them*.

→ Find ways to challenge what they believe, while presuming that they will enjoy the conversation and seeing to it that they do.

→ Presume that to get them to be flexible in their opinions, you have to be willing to be flexible in yours.

→ Expect that they will go away and think about what you said (only the rarest and most impressive people change their minds in public).

You must do more than pretend. Find something within yourself, your product or your position that really is of value *to them*. Instead of 'convincing' someone, you're believing it, getting into flow with them, and letting them feel that sense of assuredness that comes from your point of view.

Do this:
Prepare presuppositions for an upcoming challenge

Think of an approaching challenge you might face. Think of someone who has a behaviour that you want to change, someone you want to date, a job you want to get, or a sale you'd like to make.

Write out a list and include:

→ all the logistical benefits for your solution (price, distance, time, size, etc.);

→ the emotional considerations. Think about primary emotions (fear, excitement, anger).

Focus on the benefits that your solution offers, and let your confirmation bias convince you that you are right. Make it big, and real, and then speak those things out loud. See yourself making friends with the person (or people), being relaxed (or happy, or excited), and succeeding at getting them to feel positive about your solution.

Hypnotic persuasion techniques

Relax, I'm not going to ask you to dangle any watches or hypnotise anyone. We're just going to look at some of the techniques of hypnosis that can be deployed in ordinary speech.

Hypnosis is basically a verbal way of inducing states of flow in people. When you are calm, authoritative and speak simply and eloquently, with smooth, flowing words that are clear and commanding, you can draw people into relaxed and suggestible states. When we are with people we don't know well, or discussing contentious topics with people whom we might not agree, we actively sort through the things they say and wonder 'What's this guy's angle?' That critical reasoning is a private distraction, and takes up some of our consciousness, stopping us from getting into flow.

You need to encourage your listener to feel comfortable, to relax and let words wash over them, and then you can use that state of flow to lead them towards a desired outcome, whether it be to buy now, quit smoking, relax, or cluck like a chicken.

Create a 'yes' state

This is a technique that's used in sales a lot and is called The Law of 7 Yeses. When a good salesperson reaches the end of their pitch, they sum up their customer's desires and how their product's relevant features match those desires, aiming to get the buyer to say 'yes', out loud, seven times before being lead to the conclusion 'So we can get started on the paperwork now.' After agreeing so much, the final result will often seem like a natural conclusion.

'Yes' answers let us relax. You can say things that evoke yes responses by stating undeniable truths and by repeating their own words (our own words evoke a particularly strong 'YES!' response); and then start weaving in hints or instructions that move towards your desired outcome (perhaps to 'relax', 'approve this' or 'hire me'). The listener will enjoy this self-affirming experience, they'll relax and lower their critical filter, interrogating each idea less and less, becoming more likely to agree with you without really listening for the logic in what you're saying.

✔ **Do evoke yes responses:** 'As we are sitting here (yes) talking (yes) about my promotion (yes), I'm beginning to wonder (yes) about that promotion (yep), because I think I'm the perfect person for that role (okay).'

Be the authority

If we are going to hand over our critical reasoning to someone, we'll give it to someone who seems like they know what they're doing. If a man in a lab coat tells you that you may experience an 'itching sensation' before giving you a placebo, you will. A sense of authority is one of the most powerful tools of persuasion.

Exercises in The Voice gave you a variety of ways to carry yourself, speak, inflect your voice and move that exude a sense of confidence and communicate authority. When you are sure of what you're saying (and you say it well), and you inflect your sentences mindfully, other people will attach to it that same sense of certainty.

You can also give people compelling reasons to believe you, perhaps with some impressive sounding 'research' (such as the references to studies you've found littered throughout this book). Wearing a nice suit, or hanging a bunch of degrees on the wall behind you will also add to your air of authority. Speaking to someone from an elevated position with a deep, authoritative tone will also help, which is why priests drone from pulpits.

Ways to exude authority

→ You could get up from the table (ostensibly to refill your coffee cup or look out the window), so that you are standing right before you deliver a particularly important point. Be aware that from a distance this will communicate authority, but as you get closer, it'll become threatening or arousing.

→ Deciding where things go also indicates authority – and directing where people should sit in a meeting is an easy way to do this, particularly as it suggests that they're subordinate (which is why you don't tell your boss where to sit). The more instructions you can have someone follow, the better, as once they get into a pattern of following them, they'll continue to do so.

→ Speak from your gut, and use downward inflections when you want to make definite points.

→ Your body language should express comfort, openness and a calm expectation.

→ Dress well, and know your stuff. Research companies before you talk to them, read over proposals in detail before pitching them. Even if you don't end up showing your knowledge, the comfort from knowing you know it will help.

Match and lead

A good hypnotic operator (or any old orator) will start 'with' the subject, speaking at their pace, intensity and pitch, using similar language and style, talking about their current surroundings or thoughts, mirroring their current beliefs and binding those together to lead them towards the desired outcome.

Talking about the current situation or environment or facts that you know about your listener 'matches' their experience. With each statement they hear, their 'yes' state strengthens, lowering their critical filter, and bringing them further into flow with you. From there you can begin to lead them.

This effect becomes even stronger if you link matching and leading, so that it seems that one is *causing* the other.

✔ **Do causally link the two:** 'As you sit here and begin to relax' ('sitting here' is the match and 'begin to relax' is the lead).

How to use this matching and leading

When persuading people, start off on common ground, establishing how well you know one another, reminding them of past pleasant experiences, or common goals and ideals. Mirror them, dress like them, use the same words they do. They should feel progressively more comfortable around you, so when you start proposing your ideas, they seem like natural conclusions, as if they come from someone who is part of (or the leader of) the in-group.

Start meetings, job interviews or presentations with small talk and humour. Relax, bond with them. Talk about the room casually, drawing their focus to anything else that's happening: sounds from outside, the location, sunlight (if there is any, but this is the UK, so that's not likely). It's useful to mention positive, uplifting things. Don't gripe about public transport – it might match someone's experience but it leads them to a negative mindset.

Lead your listeners towards useful mindsets and outcomes using phrases like '...you're probably wondering...' followed by '...how we can make this system work well for us.' Use clean questions to find out what excites them, and bind those emotions to your solution.

The word 'because' is powerful. It suggests a causal connection, and people are inclined to relax simply knowing that it's there, often without assessing it. There was some rather amusing research by Ellen Langer in which someone asked if they could cut in front of people to use a copier at a university library, in one instance saying 'Because I have to make copies'. The study found that 93 per cent of people agreed, compared to only 60 per cent if the person said 'Excuse me,

I have five pages, may I use the Xerox™ machine?' If you look at them, the second, less successful reason is actually a more compelling reason to let someone push in front. 'Because I have to make some copies'!? Doesn't everyone in the copier queue have to make copies? The lesson? Always attach your matching statements to your ideas or instructions using the word 'because'. Why? Because, somehow, it works.

Embedded commands

Once you've created a comfortably confused state in someone, their overloaded brain searches for simplicity and meaning. As they start to reach out and grab at ideas, they should find your speech laced with simple instructions like 'relax', 'call me', 'buy it now' or 'kill the president of Burma'. They can, on the surface, appear to be part of another sentence or question. These commands simply need to be marked out in a way that the person's subconscious will 'hear' them.

You can **mark these commands** out by verbally putting them in bold, or pausing almost imperceptibly before you say them. The trick here is to inflect the sentence as a command, even though that might be unnatural. To make it an instruction or statement, it needs a downward inflection, which sounds only a tiny bit different, and might seem a bit out of place, but it makes a whole lot of difference.

'Now' is also a powerful word because it can be a suggestion or an instruction, and can fit between two complete phrases. So if someone is 'probably beginning to wonder how deeply you can **relax now**', immediately followed by '...that you are becoming aware of your breathing', it could suggest that they should start wondering, or actually going into the trance, or perhaps it's just a statement of what is actually happening. It becomes unclear whether you're describing what's going on, or it's going on because you're describing it. 'Now' is heard as both a statement about time, but also as a command: 'Act now!'

How to use embedded commands

Try to ensure the embedded command fits into your speech as a full sentence by itself

✗ **Not a full sentence:** 'So we're sitting here, talking about **giving me a raise**.'

✔ **A full sentence:** 'So as we sit here, we can talk about whether you'll **give me a raise**.'

Be sure to make these statements or commands active and definite.

✘ **Don't be wishy washy:** 'As you **consider this proposal**' is an embedded command, but 'consider' is not a very powerful instruction. Instead try:

✔ **Definite command:** 'As you consider whether to **approve this proposal**.'

Even simpler and much more effective than secretly embedding commands within your speech is to simply state them. You'll find that people actually enjoy being told what to do, when the instructions are clear and they like the instructor. When you end speeches or ask people to do things, finish with a simple command, like this one.

Predicting irrationality

There are a variety of ways in which we are predictably irrational, and these irrational quirks make us particularly easy to persuade.

When an idea is presented to us that conflicts with what we currently believe or want to believe, we experience a state of mental discomfort called cognitive dissonance. The term cognitive dissonance was first coined by a chap called Leon Festinger. He conducted a study in which he asked participants to do something really, really boring, and upon completing it they were asked to lie to other participants (actually actors) to say it was actually loads of fun (researchers are outsourcing their lies now). He paid the participants different amounts of money, and afterwards he asked them how much they had actually enjoyed the task. The results were quite surprising. He found that the less he paid them to lie, the more they claimed to have enjoyed the task. Leon's explanation was that the poorly paid students had no way to justify their lie (they'd only made $1), which caused dissonance with their cherished belief 'I am a good/honest person'. To ease the dissonance, they were inclined to believe themselves and adjust their memory of the event. The better paid group had a justification to lie – 'I just made 20 bucks!'

– so they suffered less dissonance and returned to study for their future career in banking.

We very much like to see ourselves as honest, kind and smart, which is important to remember when persuading people. Don't seek to demonstrate that someone is wrong. Let them indulge their cherished beliefs, match them, and align those comforting feelings with your goal.

We actively seek out evidence to confirm our more pleasing ideas, avoid disconfirming evidence, and find excuses to ignore it when it finds us. This is known as the confirmation bias. The confirmation bias allows us to experience illusory superiority, which makes the vast majority of us believe we are more intelligent, kind, perceptive and have a better sense of humour than most of those around us. When faced with an IQ test or disconfirming evidence, we'll excuse it by saying 'I was having a bad day' or 'I have different *kind* of intelligence'. If you're reading this and thinking 'Yes, but I really *am* above average', you're doing it right now. Don't worry. We all do.

Do this:
Challenge a long-held belief

Challenging your long and dearly held beliefs is an invaluable tool for self-development (as the more rigidly held beliefs are often the least helpful). It's a tool for persuasion because actively challenging your beliefs is a useful way to test whether what you're persuading someone to do is actually right, or just the result of these biases. Remember, due to their nature, these beliefs hide from our conscious introspection so saying 'I am not biased' is a ridiculous statement.

Think about the things you believe, and entertain for a moment that you might be wrong. Go on the internet, or find someone who disagrees with you, and boldly seek out the disconfirming evidence. Accept and challenge your desire to find weak sources, or to look at what the people on your side are saying about the other side.

This should be a challenging experience for you. If it isn't, look harder, and challenge something bigger, deeper, more closely guarded.

Being able to do this will make you a better person, with better friendships, weaker beliefs and stronger ideas.

Exploiting cognitive biases

Knowing that people see themselves as perceptive, kind and intelligent, you can make 'Barnum' statements which are broad and vague, but because they're complimentary, they'll seem quite accurate to the listener. This is how psychics work. The following statements are pleasing, and therefore will almost always evoke 'yes' responses and induce flow – provided they believe you.

→ **Use the confirmation bias:** 'You've probably noticed...'

→ **Use illusory superiority:** 'I've noticed that you are quite intelligent, so I'm sure you agree...'

→ **Use the Barnum effect:** 'You seem like someone who thinks deeply and is quite perceptive. I bet sometimes you like to sit and watch people. I reckon you have a keen intuition. Buy my dog.'

Just try to avoid calling people perceptive in front of other people you've also called perceptive. Even better, only say it when it's honest and relevant.

First things last

Each of us have a way of thinking that supports our current lifestyle, beliefs and behaviour. Be wary of what ideas you present, when and how you present them. Being abrupt or telling someone that they or something they're doing is 'wrong' will only entrench them further. The more invested someone is (financially, logistically, or in terms of identity), the more likely they are to fight back. If you want to change the way someone thinks, get to the crux of your argument last. First find your common ground. The more radical the persuasion, the more costly the purchase, the more opposed the ideology, the more effort, time, and emotion you will need to invest before you get to it.

→ Start *with* your listener. Get in flow with them, make friends and join their in-group.

→ Ask questions. Allow them to indulge their sense of self.

→ Reinforce 'yes' answers by repeating what they say and agreeing with them (when you really do agree with them).

→ Instead of arguing facts, search for a good reason for them to *want* to agree.

...and *then* share your ideas with them.

Encourage people to express their support

Our opinions are usually malleable until we state them publicly. If people are likely to disagree, avoid letting them express their doubts. When talking to a crowd, keep an eye out for sparkling eyes and nodding heads. When you can see that people support you, encourage them to speak up. Get them to expand on your points or ask them how they feel about the idea. As an in-group bias sets in, and you get the group in flow, the hold-outs' desire to belong will bring them along (which is much easier if they've not yet stated their objection). This is why con-artists and street salesmen will often have a plant who pretends to be an ordinary punter and is the first to loudly express their excitement at such a great offer.

Let them devise reasons why your goal will work, or ways to improve it, which they will believe, and therefore support.

→ **Ask them:** 'How could we make this work better?'

→ **Ask them:** 'So you think that might work? Great. **What do you think are the advantages of this approach?**'

And as always, repeat their words back to them. It will cement them in their memory as something they have said and believe.

Get them to take the first step

Have you ever had to describe a card game to someone? It always sounds boring, no matter how exciting the game turns out to be. Get them to start playing, however, and they'll soon realise it's enjoyable. Remember Leon Festinger's boredom experiment. If you want to get someone to do something, don't start with an explanation. Get them started, pay them nothing, and let them explain to themselves why they're doing it.

✗ **Don't explain:** 'If you want to repeat an order you would log on...'

✔ **Do get going:** 'I've brought a demo. To log on, click there...'

Accept other people's help

If someone has already helped you work towards something, they'll feel bonded to you and invested in the outcome. If you work together, physically doing the same demanding task, the parallel focus will draw you into flow with one another. When you then share your views, they will be taken on board and valued more highly. There is also a self-affirming meaning attached to those moments for the person who's helping you: 'I am a good person', 'I am good at this'.

You can also get them to talk towards your goal.

✗ **Don't decide for yourself:** 'Should parliament ban live meat exports?'

✔ **Do get going:** 'So how would you go about getting parliament to ban live meat exports?'

✔✔ **Even better:** 'Can you come up with reasons why parliament should ban live meat exports?'

Create constraints

Humans tend to be loss averse and hate missing out. If your product or service is always available, then there is no incentive to 'act now' because it's 'for a limited time only'. Not realising this is what causes people to complain about being 'friend zoned', because they are permanently 'there for' someone, so there isn't an incentive to act. The same goes for job offers. If you're happy to come and work for someone 'whenever', they're less likely to call you, ever. Make it clear that you have options and they'll feel lucky to have you. Similarly, as a freelancer or consultant, don't always be available. Set boundaries and bend them only in extreme circumstances, and when people do have your business or attention, they'll value it more highly.

Be careful giving away freebies

When I have allowed people to attend my workshops for free, I've had to work twice as hard for their participation. They invest less into each exercise, take less from it, and at the end of the day they're more likely to say it was pointless. A full-paying person sitting next to them will report having had a 'life changing experience' and often say they would have been willing to pay more. Many businesses report similar effects when they increase the price of their products or suddenly make their services less available: they immediately seem more valuable. The best seductions allow both lovers to maintain the illusion that they did all the work. The harder we work for things, the more we value them, so avoid giving away freebies.

Now, in contradictory fashion…

Give a bit

When asking something of someone, start out with an act of kindness. We have biological hard-wiring for reciprocity, which causes us to feel uncomfortable when someone gives us a nicer Christmas or birthday present than we gave them. Give away discounts, sweets, and insightful, heartfelt compliments, and people will feel that they owe you.

Many salespeople conspiratorially offer 'special' discounts 'just 'cos I like you', and sweets in the tray with your bill at dinner will make you give bigger tips. It's up to you to find the balance between giving too much and not enough.

Other points on persuasion

Respect their autonomy

We see ourselves as logical and free-willed, so we're repelled at the idea of being persuaded. That is what makes persuasion such a subtle art. Where you can, give people some room. We get very anxious about the 'road not taken', and often see deciding on one thing as deciding against the other. Whenever you can, leave the choices on the table. A time constraint or other pressure can motivate people in your absence ('I will need to know by the end of the day').

If you're persuading someone to change their opinion or hire you, giving them space to let them decide can demonstrate your value more than a permanent, pestering presence. When it comes to personal values, religious beliefs or political persuasions, people will change these at a glacial pace, and rarely, if ever, change them in public. Give them time and space, and be nice about it.

Be persistent

Respecting people's autonomy doesn't mean pitching something once and running for the hills. Be persistent and friendly. Make an effort to ensure your interactions are enjoyable, and people won't mind you calling them up every now and then. As you build a friendship and a solid working relationship with someone, you'll be at the front of their mind when that next job comes up, or they need something that you have to offer.

Seek feedback from them. Ask them plainly, or crack jokes about being too persistent. They will give feedback with their responses. If they don't mind, they'll go to lengths to say so.

Be flexible and reasonable

Be willing to admit when you're wrong. It's one of the most generous things you can do. It shows respect to the other person and sets an example. And, being able to accept when you're wrong is the surest route to being right. What's more, others will see it as an act of giving. They will want to reciprocate and change their views, to match you, and get that feeling of freedom that comes from changing what you believe.

The more flexible you are with what makes you happy, the more likely you are to be happy. People enjoy having options, and they enjoy feeling that they had an impact – give them a variety of ways to please you and they'll enjoy the outcome too.

- ✗ **Don't have an intractable position:** 'This is how it must be done.'
- ✔ **Do workshop the result:** 'Good point. How else could we do it?'

The value of vulnerability

Too often we see being 'confident', 'independent' and 'certain' as something aspirational. We want to stand on our own two feet, and be seen to be doing so. It's understandable. Vulnerability is a scary concept. It evokes images of dependence and suggests weakness. But on our own, we are weak. We are social creatures. Interdependence is exactly what makes us, as a species, so strong. We need to feel needed.

If you ask for advice, take it on board. If it wasn't asked for, you can still thank them kindly and decide for yourself. Be willing to be proven wrong. Admit your mistakes. Allow people to laugh at you.

- ✗ **Don't say you are unnecessary to me:** 'I'll figure it out. I don't need your help.'
- ✔ **Do say you are important to me:** 'I would love to hear your thoughts.'
- ✔ **Do say your ideas influence my thinking:** 'That's a great point. I hadn't thought of that.'

Strike that balance between being vulnerable and being a moaner. It's the same as the balance between confidence and arrogance – it must authentic and useful. Be authentic, open up to people, and do it for a purpose.

Do this:
Share your weakness, show your strength

Build rapport with someone by sharing a weakness. When you are next around someone who you don't know very well, or aren't on the best of terms with, talk about your vulnerability. It's scary, yes. All the worthwhile things are. Get into a normal conversation and then be serious, honest, and share with them a fear you have. It must be real, and you must let it affect you.

Keep in mind that you are not imposing this upon them, but sharing it with them. It can be a universal fear that's easily relatable ('I don't know if you've ever felt like you're an impostor waiting to get found out'). It will be a moment when you are vulnerable in a real, emotional sense, and that's the way it should be.

Self-deprecation is effective for building rapport, but it's only really funny when we know that it's coming from a place of strength. The post clerk cracking jokes about their disastrous date is just sad. If the boss does it, it's hilarious.

Ask them!

Save the most effective strategy until last, and it's devastatingly simple. Just ask them!

→ **'What would convince you?'** will evoke rational responses, which can be good to establish whether anything would.

→ **'What are you looking for?'** will give more off-the-cuff gut responses.

→ **'How would you feel if... ?'** is a great one for finding an emotional trigger that motivates people, which can be followed with...

→ **'What would work for you?'** will give them options to answer.

Their answer won't always be useful, even if it's honest (people with emotional beliefs often give logical requirements, which, once answered, still fail to convince them), but many times it will be as simple as answering their needs.

Once you've asked the question, people will start persuading themselves. Upon telling you what it would take, they will feel bound by their own words, making them much more likely to follow through. It's amazing how rarely the 'What would it take?' question is asked, given how powerful it is.

Do this:

Persuade someone to do something

Convince someone to do something (not just change what they think, it should be something they must do).

→ Make friends with them.

→ If you think they might not be averse to it, present your idea to them. ▶

→ Ask them questions about what they value and what they want from life.

→ Ask them what it would take to get them to do it.

→ Weave their words into what you're saying, create a 'yes' state, and match and lead them towards the outcome.

→ Get them to start making steps towards the goal, just to 'see how it feels'.

→ Get them to describe the advantages, and how they feel now in positive terms.

Ask them how they enjoyed the experience of being persuaded. Notice how they respond to the idea of having been 'persuaded'.

Storytelling

Chapter Eight

When we developed vocal chords, we grew a neural hard-wiring that makes us yearn to tell stories and love listening to them. Stories allow others to learn from our mistakes, to discover which tribes are friendly and which berries are poisonous. Think of those times when something weird happens and you feel as if you're bursting to share it with someone; or those times when you've been transported by someone's tale and lost yourself in their telling of it.

Make your stories rich and immersive, so they transport people through time and space, and the vivid thoughts and feelings that you create will transport your listener in a way that mere facts cannot. Stories share information, experience, and offer new perspectives. Fill your presentations, persuasive discussions, pitches and interviews with stories of past challenges, victories and bittersweet memories. Run your pitches as if they're a story. Use stories to motivate others, describing old challenges and how they were overcome.

Story structure

Every pitch, every presentation, even every campaign to persuade someone should be told as if it's a fascinating story that must be told. When we hear a story, we are drawn in, and feel as if we need to be there until the end. Far too often people waste time introducing what they're going to say when it's totally unnecessary, just like asking someone if you can ask them a question. Get on with it! Rather than saying what you're going to say, tell them *why* you're saying it. Get their attention, change how they feel, and tell them what to do.

Get their attention

Start your story with something attention-grabbing. A hint at the final punchline or moral can be good, particularly if it doesn't ruin the gist of the story. Otherwise, just start off big, in a style that clearly indicates a story is being told. Don't undermine your point, self-deflate or excuse yourself, as if you're apologising for speaking before you've even spoken. Avoid even introducing it – launch straight into it.

'**So there I was**, sitting atop this huge black horse, surrounded by men with guns...'

Change how they feel

Tell your story. Make sure every element is essential, engaging, and clearly described (rather than explained). Remember, stories should not just share information, they should share an experience. Wherever you can, show rather than tell. Act bits out in a minimal way if you want. Your story should be just long enough to get all the points across, and just a bit shorter than your listener wants it to be.

Tell them what to do

If it's just a story, you can end it with a moral or a punchline. If it's a punchline that requires a particular wording to be funny, avoid using that word in the set-up of the story. Either way, finish on a high, and then let someone else speak. If your story is long enough, they'll comment 'Oh that's amazing'; if they want more, they'll ask 'What happened next?'

Some points on story style

Engage your audience – talk to them, not at them. Talk to people about experiences in which they will be interested. People who don't like bikes or travelling won't listen to 'this time I went travelling on my bike' stories, unless you tell it well and include a lot of references to experiences which they will have shared or ideas they do care about. If someone has an experience or knowledge that is relevant to your story, engage them with that element. You can say 'You know what it's like to get caught in a blizzard, don't you Agnes?' and hand the story over to her to explain that part. Sharing attention is a generous thing to do, and makes people feel more inclined to let their focus come back to you. They will have an excitement and mild nervousness that they might be called upon next, which will ensure they follow each detail closely.

Directing people's attention like this is a very, very useful technique in storytelling, and denotes power at work, in meetings and in all aspects of social life. Casting these beams of attention among a group will establish you as a leader. Even people who are too shy to take the spotlight will enjoy basking in attention when it's given to them in this way. We appreciate balance when attention is shared, and when we're getting it, we don't care who's steering. It's also an interesting insight – if you want to know who's leading a group, wait for a pause and notice where everyone looks. If they all look at you, you're the boss. You can steer conversation by directing the attention towards certain people or topics, driving it towards happy, fun, and useful discussion (and away from talking recursively about boring, upsetting, or socially exclusive topics).

Create a rich sensory experience. Describe how the wind whistled as it whipped your hair, using assonance and onomatopoeia to describe how as it blew, it tugged, snapped and flapped at your coat. Talk about the chill of the salty breeze that blew off the ocean's white-capped waves. Describe her hair, the warmth of his arms, and the softness in her eyes, how they were warm and wet, and how they held each other close. The richer and more engaging your stories, the more they will affect changes in your listener. Listeners will start to see and hear the scene, and smell the smells. If you scanned their brain, their visual, auditory and olfactory sensors will be reacting almost as if the stimuli were real. These can make for rich metaphors, which spur people to action or urge caution in a way that is much more visceral and effective than simply being told. Simple or common experiences need fewer details to communicate the story effectively, but even these stories can be improved with rich details.

Elicit an emotional response from your listener. First, know what you want that response to be. Know who is the audience's protagonist. It may not be you, even though you're the one telling the tale. Know what kind of emotions you're summoning, and be sure to know why you're summoning them. Don't tell a story about heartbreak on a date, and don't tell a story about a catastrophic failure on the pitch.

Know when your story ends. Be short. Before you start telling a tale, know why you're telling it and that will tell you where it should end. Mentally work backwards from there to include only the relevant details. Finish with a punchline, a big reveal, or even with a moral: 'The moral of this story is you should never poke a crab unless you're sure it's dead.' End it however you want, but for God's sake, end it.

Speak for Yourself

Balance investment with reward. Bear in mind what the audience is getting from the story – the funnier it is, or the bigger the point, the longer it can be. We don't want to listen to an hour-long story if it's 'just a point about that thing you just said'. If the story is going to be hilarious, it can go for a bit longer, but please, include other funny or interesting moments along the way!

Be keenly aware of how engaged your audience is. It can be easy to get caught up in the telling of a story and not notice how it is affecting your audience. Keep your eyes on your listeners and notice if they start to fidget, look around or check the time. If your listeners are aware of distractions (or actively looking for them), that's an obvious sign they aren't interested. If they are tuning out, engage them or finish fast. If there is still a long way to go, perhaps abandon the story altogether. I often use the line 'Wow! I just realised how boring this is, I'm going to stop talking now.' I find it is very effective at bringing people back on-side with a bit of laughter.

Boast only if it's an essential detail. People hate to hear boasting because it seems as if you simultaneously consider yourself better than your listener *while* desperately seeking their approval. People would far prefer to hear you being self-deprecating and *learning*, rather than just being. If your story is 'I was so great at something, and everyone thought I was so attractive', then just don't tell it. If details about your looks, skills or privileged birthright are important to the telling of a tale, share those details briefly and get on with the story.

But don't trash yourself either. When telling a story about yourself, there is an important balance that needs to be struck between telling necessary details, to self-deprecating, down to just trashing yourself. It's a spectrum. At the trashing yourself end, people will feel that it is their duty to interrupt your story and make you feel better. In the sweet spot, you should demonstrate sufficient humility and self-awareness to make your self-deprecation endearing and funny. With every listener, this sweet spot will be different. Each listener and their current self-perception will change what they want to listen to. It is up to you to continually calibrate and adjust your story.

Don't get involved in one-upmanship anecdote tennis. It can be enticing, but that game has many losers and few winners. The problem is that as they escalate, each person is more focused on telling their story rather than hearing each other's. This makes for an audience who isn't so much receptive as waiting for their turn to talk (sometimes even taking breath each time another person pauses, so desperate are they to get to speak). The escalation will also cause people to embellish details or flat out lie to make their tale match the curve. It also means that as each story is told, the previous tellers feel as if they have been outdone; so that even the ultimate winner doesn't so much tell a great story, as effectively end the game for everyone else. Sit, listen, laugh, ask questions, and try as hard as you can to abstain.

Job interview stories

In job interviews, you are being asked to list your greater qualities. We all hate doing this, with the exception of people who are unreasonably positive in their self-assessment. Tell stories that demonstrate your skills and how you learned them, and you'll get around having to make irksome lists of your positive attributes. Draw similarities between past experiences and the ones ahead of you in the role, and then you can quite explicitly highlight your strengths.

- ✗ **Don't make statements:** 'I'm a fast learner' (all applicants say that, particularly those who are hopelessly under-qualified).
- ✔ **Do tell a story with a point:** 'What I learned from that experience is that it is more important to make people want to do things than simply telling them they have to. I guess I already knew that, but I learned *how* to do that.'

Stories also allow you to admit to failings and present them as strengths. Interviewers are looking for ability, but they're also looking for humanity. They are deciding who they're going to be hanging out with for eight hours every day. If you demonstrate that you're funny, modest, perceptive and fun to hang out with, they'll *want* to hire you, and you can leave it up to them to explain why.

Sales stories

When you've asked clean questions, learned all of the customer's decision criteria and their words, and their emotional triggers, then tie them up in the conclusion of a sales story.

Speak for Yourself

✔ **Do tell a story using their words:** 'I want to be sure that when you're walking out the door, you <u>feel that freedom</u> of having <u>the wind against your face</u> as you ride down the road on your new motorbike.'

Build up an imaginary scenario of whatever gets them going, and they'll feel transported into a fantasy world in which they have your product. When the story evaporates and leaves them back in reality, without your product, they'll feel as if they lost it. Now they'll really want it.

It can also be effective to describe previous customers who were in similar situations (budget restrictions, schedules, etc.) and how they were apprehensive, and then lead through to their conclusion. Notice the following difference, supposing your customer wants peace of mind.

✘ **Don't make the statement:** 'Don't worry, I'll handle it' (feels like a brush-off).

✔ **Do tell a story:** '...she is in Jamaica, lying on the beach, and actually called yesterday to tell me that she was so glad I'd <u>handled it all</u>, so she could just **relax now**' (with <u>their words</u> and an **embedded command**).

Do this:
Tell a story

Next time you're presenting an idea, tell a story. Find something that happened to you, that in some way relates to what you're saying. Tell it, and get as invested in the art of telling it as you can. Adjust your voice to match the pace, style and content, and finish with a metaphor and a call to arms.

Speak in metaphors

Metaphors are powerful because they expose new ways of thinking, offering perspective and insight. They summon images, colours, sounds and memories within our imagination, each of which can evoke powerful emotions that hold the power to change people. The richer, more relatable, memorable and emotive these ideas are, the more powerful they become.

I had a client who was going to give a talk on a 'client engagement protocol' and was recommending that the company he worked for invest money and time into building a system that the clients could interact with, which would encourage them to keep spending money. As is so often in corporate structures, the people in charge of deciding whether to implement a system were a long way from the people who would eventually use it, and thus had little understanding of what it was or why it was needed. In truth, I didn't really understand the whole idea either, so I asked him to explain it in a metaphor. He did:

> **We're in a long-distance relationship** and our clients are our girlfriend. We're sitting here occasionally calling her up and chatting with her, but she's getting bored. Other men are calling her with offers. They sometimes drop by her house with flowers. We've got to keep her interest or her eye will wander!

Bam. Suddenly it was real and far more interesting than a 'client engagement protocol' – it's something we all understand. This girlfriend has value, she's sexy, just like our client who's sexy because they're spending money. Other businesses want our clients as surely as other men want my girlfriend. It's the way the world is. What's more, it's funny. Barely five minutes into his presentation, his project was approved.

Metaphors are also useful for explaining interpersonal dynamics for someone who is stuck inside a situation. Emotions and desires can cloud our perception, making it difficult for us to understand other people's motivation (aside from 'because he's an idiot!'). Trying to explain another person's behaviour to someone who is upset can often result in arguing with your friend on behalf of someone you've never even met. Metaphors allow you to illuminate a situation, and other people's motivations, from a safer ground. Metaphors offer perspective.

It can also be interesting to look at things as if they already are a metaphor. If someone covers their mouth when they laugh, what does that say about their outlook on life?

Points on metaphor

→ You don't need to go with your first idea – test out a few to find one that works.

→ Make it immersive, visual, and with a clear point.

→ A metaphor should have legs. When you set it free, you should find that it continues to describe the situation more and more clearly. It will often become quite funny, and will be much more memorable.

→ The constructed metaphor should be totally removed from what it's describing, or it'll muddy itself by needing to describe itself all over again.

   ✗ **Not removed:** 'Think of the computer file structure like your email inbox, where files are like emails, and can be saved in different folders.'

   ✔ **Removed:** 'Think of your computer file structure like a car park. You have to remember where you parked your car.'

→ It can (and sometimes *should*) be whimsical as metaphors often evoke a childlike state, but it must retain an inherent logic.

   ✔ **Inherent logic:** 'So this little duck never quacks. How is she going to find a boy-duck to fall in love with?'

   ✗ **Lacking inherent logic** 'So the little duck doesn't have a hammer. How is it going to build a barn?'

Postscript: I'm aware I'm mostly talking about similes, and referring to them as metaphors. Leave me alone. I don't use it because I don't like how that word is spelled.

Do this:
Create a metaphor

Think of a concept in your work (or perhaps something technical from a hobby) that would be quite difficult to explain to a layperson (perhaps use an example you've struggled to explain in the past). Spend some time daydreaming, and devise a metaphor to explain how it works or what needs doing.

Public speaking

Chapter Nine

There is a common belief that people fear public speaking more than they fear death, which is utter hogwash. The source of this oft-misquoted claim probably comes from a study done in 1973, found in the 1977 edition of *The Book of Lists,* in which people were surveyed about what they feared most.

Public speaking came in first place with 41 per cent of participants listing it, though they were able to list more than one fear. That was followed by heights, then insects and bugs, financial problems, then deep water, sickness *and then* death; followed by other fears such as loneliness, dogs and escalators. That doesn't mean people fear it *more* than they fear death (to test that idea, perhaps you could hold a gun to someone's head, ask them to speak, and see how they respond). All this study tells us is that when you say 'What are you afraid of?' public speaking is the first thing that comes to many minds. Even so, the results are quite revealing.

If you look over that list, you'll see that all of the other fears are quite rational. Evolutionary selection is at work to ensure that we are afraid of bugs (which are often poisonous). The same goes for heights. 'Financial problems' is the modern equivalent of a fear of starvation. Deep water and sickness also kill us. Loneliness, to a tribal human, would spell death. The only item on that list which couldn't threaten one's mortal safety is public speaking. So why is it such a common fear?

I suspect that we have evolved with a fear of public speaking because it self-selects for leadership. The strongest early tribes would have been those who bonded and worked towards common goals, and that takes leadership. A fear of speaking thins out the numbers of people willing to stand on a rock and tell people what to do – and fewer leaders means clearer leadership. It goes further. Good leaders are calm. When under pressure, effective leaders are the people who can control their emotions, think clearly and speak simply. An ingrained fear of speaking ensures that people who are ruled by their emotions are precluded from sharing their fearful ideas. The people who master their fear are able to lead people, and their calm ideas will be easily followed. That put tribes who feared public speaking at a survival advantage over competing tribes who were a cacophony of confident loudmouths.

Do not for a moment think you can give me this 'some people are born with it' baloney. That is only ever said by people who believe they were born without 'it'. Those who were born with it, without exception, will tell you how terrified they were the first 20 or 30 times they did it, how they kept at it, developed their skill and mastered their nerves and eventually became quite good at it. Confidence and a feeling of assuredness come from experience. Get more experience at public speaking, and you'll feel more confident.

Please speak up. Confidence correlates so poorly with morality, we need more people to speak up. Speak up, not 'even though' it's scary; speak up *because* it's scary. As your body gets used to the experience, your cortisol levels will normalise, the fear will subside, and a useful excitement will remain.

Preparing a speech

Set a goal

Decide on your goal for the speech. Ask yourself 'What do I want to achieve?' It should be positive, forward thinking and active. Every word, every movement, and every detail of your speech will be directed towards that single clear purpose, and your audience needs to know it. Tell them from the start: 'At the end of this talk, I will ask you to...' so they know why they're listening.

If you've got to explain a new system, then 'explaining a new system' isn't active, isn't very exciting, nor is it a valid reason to speak, so we won't really listen. Getting excited and using this new system is much more useful, and understanding is required for that enthusiasm, so explaining is something you'll do in pursuit of your goal. The more excited they are, the more likely they will be to act.

Set a purpose

Define your purpose. When your goal is rooted in some deep, personal purpose, it will evoke in you a passion that will infect others. Seek to improve the lives of your listeners, so that they may improve the lives of others; encourage rational enquiry and free thinking; change the world; unseat dictators and protect the innocent. You decide. We'll focus on defining that purpose at the end of the book, but it pays to start thinking about it now. Ask yourself: 'What do I stand for?'

Get passionate

The more ambitious your purpose, the stronger the urge to speak. Allow yourself to speak loudly, clearly, and emote freely with authenticity. As you get more and more driven towards your purpose, you become more fascinating, and as you fall into a state of flow, you'll draw your audience along towards your immediate goal.

Structure your speech

Setting your clear, active, solution-oriented goal will tell you what you need to talk about, helping you to cut out bits that may be interesting but are irrelevant. Your goal will give a narrative to your structure. Fit it into the following three parts.

1 Get their **attention**.

- Tell them your goal as a teaser: 'I'm going to ask you to do three things...'

- Hint at the ending: 'I'm going to tell you a story about why puppies are evil' or:

- Launch into a story: 'I was adrift on a boat with no petrol, no GPS, and a broken mast in the middle of the Atlantic Ocean, thinking to myself...'

2 Change how they **feel**

- Lay out logical arguments, using 'because' and 'so', so that the causes between them are obvious. Explain complex points and get emotional investment using metaphors.

- Focus on bright futures, fun, humour and interesting ideas; all of it leading towards your goal.

- Revise the earlier section on persuasion for making these points effective.

3 Issue a clear **instruction**.

- It should be something people can do, or start doing, before the end of that day. Issue it as a command (not a question or an invitation):

  'Send me an email.'

'Ask me a question.'

'Buy my dog.'

Do it from memory

Once you've set the order of your speech, memorise it. It's boring watching people read, we always end up thinking 'Couldn't you have just emailed this to me?'. Keep a sheet of paper nearby with any crucial information on it, statistics you might be quizzed on, for example, and another *single page* with your structure written out, just in case you get lost.

Rote learning

You can learn your speech by rote. Do it over, and over, and over. This can be useful for learning lines or scripts that are set in stone. Rote learning is less desirable because it takes a long time to learn and it's inflexible, so making alterations to your speech can be difficult.

The link system

I prefer a mnemonic technique called the link system, which can be found in many memory books and resources online. Here's a brief rundown of how it works.

Consider your main points and think of some sub-headings for each. When you have the rough structure, turn each of those topics of discussion into a vivid and weird mental picture of something. Start with the first topic and move through each one, causally linking each image to the following one. Each of these mental pictures can be linked to other, finer details along the way. As long as the images are vivid (it helps if they're silly), and causally linked to one another (so each image causes or somehow affects the next, rather than just sitting next to it), you'll remember them.

For example if it's about 'process efficiency', I might imagine a huge meat-mincer processing something. If the next point is about how this efficiency makes money, imagine that the meat mincer is taking in giblets of meat but churning out shiny gold coins which are clattering into a metal tray, making a sound like a poker machine paying out. If you realise later that you should talk about Jeanette who works in accounts, go back and alter the image, actually see yourself scrub out the previous link somehow (I often do this violently, maybe I'm weird), and add a new one. Now Jeanette, dressed as an organ grinder, is turning the handle. Each image reminds you of Jeanette, of process efficiency, of budget.

Practise your speech all the way through, from memory, and whenever you stumble over a section, revisit that link, which you'll find was probably not clear or crazy enough. Make it clearer and crazier so you can remember it. Rehearsing it will remind you of the links and make them stronger. Now, try starting from the middle; then try giving the speech backwards. You'll find that with this method, you can't get lost and it's a lot easier to stop and explain things better, answer questions, talk with your audience, or return to previous points (when you do, stick a 'flag' in the point you were on so you can return to it. See yourself removing the flag each time, or it'll end up full of them).

Deliver the speech slightly differently each time, keeping it alive in your mind. With your hands, eyes and brain free from reading notes, you'll be much more compelling and responsive to your audience.

Get in a good headspace

Before your speech, do some belly breathing and remind yourself to speak from your gut. Stand up straight and test out your voice. As you breathe low and slow through your nose, focus on what you do know, and all of the things that can go well. If you think 'Have I forgotten it?' you will forget it. If you do, remember that memory is like a bar of soap. If you grip it tightly, it'll pop out of your hands. If you drop it, relax, find it, and pick it up again gently. If you panic it'll just start pinging around the bathtub. Similarly, if you think 'This is boring', your audience will get into flow with you and with that mental state, and it will be boring.

Don't focus on your nerves. If you talk about them or focus on them, you're acknowledging them and they will only get worse. This is where having a clear objective will help:

→ **Think:** 'This is exciting.'
→ **Think:** 'This must be said.'

→ **Think:** 'These ideas are important.'

→ **Think:** 'How can I say this well?'

Try to focus on doing it *well* rather than getting it *right*. 'Right' damages our creativity because there's only one right way, 'well' can be done a multitude of ways.

Visualise

See yourself doing the talk exactly as you'd like to do it, so that you develop a really rich, multi-sensory experience of having already done it. Imagine stuff-ups, technical problems and prickly questions, and see, hear, feel and even *smell* yourself handling them all with poise. Imagine finishing your talk, and people enjoying it, and you feeling excited and happy throughout. A feeling of 'I've already done this' can really help.

Practise, in front of a mirror

Become really familiar with what you're saying and the order in which you're saying it. Practise explaining concepts in different ways. Talk to yourself, in an engaging way, and get excited about what you're saying. Keep your posture fluid and erect, your voice full, rich and musical. Give yourself a rich experience of delivering this speech persuasively.

Focus on what you did well

Recap mindfully. Be aware that these thoughts soon after it will affect your memory of the event. When you have given your talk, there's a temptation to focus on the bits you forgot to say, the times you stumbled, or the things that went wrong. Focus instead on the fact that you did it, that you got your message out, and how much you improved. Focusing on these will give you memories of having done it well, making them easy to recall when you're next given an opportunity to speak. Eventually, rather than waiting to be given them, you'll make opportunities for yourself.

Gesture

'What should I do with my hands?' is a major challenge for many in public speaking. Use them, but use them *deliberately*. Your hands, fingers, arms, wrists, shoulders, body and even your legs can make points, can separate ideas or meld them together, or indicate a change in tone. The more expressively and purposefully you use your body while you speak, the more fascinating you become, and the more easily your audience will fall into flow.

Clear gestures

When discussing concepts, mark them out in space *as* something (this gets a lot easier if you describe them with a metaphor). When you're talking about opening something, *open it* with your hands. Use recognisable, clear gestures, even when discussing abstract concepts or non-physical entities, for example, to 'move them aside', 'close' them, 'open' them or 'join' them together. Pinch your fingers to a point to describe the fine grain detail of something, or point your finger if you're making a point, though try not to point at people. If you do need to point at people, an open hand, palm up, with your fingers together is a nice, welcoming gesture. Turning the same hand over will encourage them to be quiet. You can use this to invite discussion and close it again when you want to talk. Your gestures should be working to make everything you say clearer, building images and making your speech more memorable.

Pick it and stick it

Think about some of your favourite speakers again, and notice what they do with their hands and face (and even whole body) during and after they make a gesture. Good speakers do what was described to me as 'pick it and stick it' – make your gesture and hold that pose, not moving again until you have something else to do.

Most of us make flappy, wobbly, vague gestures, with our hands in constant motion or always returning to their 'home' at our sides or clasped together, only marking out the intended idea for a fleeting moment. Watch yourself in the mirror and you'll see the difference.

When you're showing that something is 'over there', point to over there, and keep your hand there until it has something else to do. The same goes for every other movement. Make it, and keep your hands there and your body in that shape, until you have a reason to move. It communicates a sense of clarity, certainty and strength.

Fit the frame

Imagine you're being watched like a film. The distance from you to your listener is relative to the size of the frame. When you're right up in someone's face, you're in an extreme close-up. Tiny facial expressions seem huge, even small hand gestures come from out of shot and seem strange or scary. The further you move away from your audience, the smaller you are in the frame, and the larger your expressions need to be to use that space. If there's 10 of you and you're in a room, open your gestures up, and speak more loudly to fill that space. If it's 100, or 1000 people, you'll need to increase your use of space accordingly. The further you are from people, the more expressive and clear you should be, and the more you can move about on stage.

Walk around or stay still?

Another tough one. It depends on the speech, but generally, I'd favour movement. Again, it should be deliberate. Don't just pace – it'll come across as nervousness and it's distracting. Focus on what you're doing when you move. Speak only when you're standing still. You can move while talking only if what you're saying is meaningless filler (which would cause one to question whether it needs saying at all). Otherwise you can use a phrase like 'But if we go back to talk about the budget...'

When you're delivering important messages that you want to stick in the mind of the listener, stop moving, look at your audience, use a firm tone, and stand stock still while you say them. They'll feel more concrete, and your words will have a whole lot more impact.

Spatial and physical anchoring

Locate your ideas within space, at a place on your stage, and even in a posture or tone of voice. When you return to that idea, return to that place, posture or tone. If you talk about the budget, place it somewhere, and come back to that when you talk about it. This method of conceptualising the elements of your speech can clarify things wonderfully in a listener's mind. Practise this when you're rehearsing your speech (which you should always do). It'll help you memorise what you're saying, and set your speech into a structure. It will also aid retention for the audience; Eddie Izzard is great at this, giving clear spaces, postures and voices to each different idea, so that once established he can weave them together quite brilliantly.

Talk to them, not at them (again)

Speak to your audience. If you can, get them to speak. Do whatever you can to have them engaged and involved in the process, and they'll be invested in the outcome. Their input will help make it interesting, give you time to collect yourself, and the whole process will be much more enjoyable. Get people to respond to you in some way, often by asking them questions, or at the very least by raising their hands. If someone appears to disagree with something you're saying, ask them questions and take their answers on board. Be open and accepting, favouring questions over arguments (arguing with them will only encourage them to argue back).

Field questions during your speech as well as at the end. Be sure to stay on track with your goal, offering to discuss things further in private when you need to get back to the point. When people agree with you, getting them to enunciate that agreement will start a social pressure, encouraging others to agree. If you mediate it well, the people who are on board with you can speak directly to those who are not.

Finish with a clear instruction

Imagine you're a fearless military leader giving a rousing speech before battle. Your call to arms does not include 'consider' or the awful 'So... Yeah. We'd like it if you could think about it, because... It's a good idea. We think'. It might sound ridiculous, but that's how many presentations end. End it strongly! If you've given a presentation, finish with a clear and easy-to-follow command such as: 'We need to communicate better between our teams. Please. <u>Talk to us</u>.' It should also be something that people can start doing immediately; if you must, create a small step that they can take before the end of that day. The command explains why you were speaking, and should have been iterated frequently within your presentation. No one should ever leave your presentation wondering why you were speaking.

Being 'professional' and having a 'presenter mode'

I can't tell you how many people I meet who have a 'professional' personality and a 'normal' them, or have a way of having a chat or speaking passionately, and a totally different 'presenter' mode when they give a speech. Please, bring your personality to work! I don't know how it happened or where this idea of a cardboard cut-out successful business person came from, but please, cut it out.

Be funny, be friendly, be open and honest, and for goodness sake, be *you*!

Other points on public speaking

→ Arrive early, get to know everyone: people will be much more 'on side' if you've already met them and introduced yourself. Arrive first and welcome each person. Ask a few questions, get to know them. Direct your points to the relevant people, by name if you can.

→ Start strong: crack out your big voice from the start as people will have done 90 per cent of their judging of you in the first 10 seconds.

→ Introduce yourself and your purpose for speaking: 'This is why I'm talking' (i.e what I want), *not* just 'This is what I'm going to talk about.'

→ Make a joke early on: as the crowd will be a bit tense, and you may be too. Break the tension early with a bit of laughter. Obviously, nothing off-colour nor anything too self-deprecating or you'll undermine your authority from the start.

→ Tell stories and use metaphors: stories make things personal and metaphors make things easy to understand. They're infinitely easier to listen to than someone babbling statistics and facts at you.

→ People love short speeches. Say as little as possible. If you've been told to speak for 20 minutes, check to see if that's essential (if you're scheduled with speakers before and after you, you may have to speak for that long). Generally, 20 minutes is the upper limit of anyone's focus. If you're forced upon pain of death into speaking for 40 minutes or more, be sure to break it up with activities, a video, or something, *anything*. Even the best orators will struggle to keep people's attention for that long.

Do this:

Take or make an opportunity to speak

Public speaking is an invaluable skill – simply knowing that you can do it and recently having done it will change how you feel about yourself. New challenges will seem exciting; more opportunities present themselves, and you'll recognise them as opportunities.

If a talk needs to be given at work, jump at it. Give a speech at a wedding, birthday or anniversary. Join a Toastmasters, or if you're really courageous, do some stand-up comedy.

Checking in: so how are you doing with all that?

So you should have practised and experienced a few states of flow lately, and played with inducing them in others. Hopefully, you're now experimenting a lot when you're at work or out and about, playing with

Speak for Yourself

ways to effect changes in other people. Here's a list of some of what we've covered in this section.

→ Getting in flow, yourself and with others.

→ **Enunciating words clearly** to draw people into flow.

→ Mirroring, subtly, to build rapport with people.

→ Noticing when people are subconsciously mirroring you.

→ Using clean language to ask questions like '**...in what way?**' to remove your presuppositions from a discussion.

→ **Copying people's wording** to create compelling statements.

→ Creating 'yes' states.

→ Some techniques of hypnosis, particularly **being the authority, matching and leading**, and **embedded commands**.

→ Telling **stories** like a pro, making them **rich, immersive and moving**.

→ Using metaphors to explain interpersonal situations or difficult concepts.

→ **Taking at least *one* opportunity to speak in public**.

→ Focusing on how well it went, and spurring yourself to do it again.

→ Learning a bunch of persuasive techniques, particularly focusing on **what you want**, while being **flexible, exciting useful feelings,** and **asking people what would influence their decision**.

In some cases, you may have felt that certain techniques, of hypnotic speech or telling rich stories perhaps, were 'too obvious' or a bit weird and decided not to use them. I recommend you go back and try using them because you may be surprised to find that people don't notice as much as you think they might (we think our quirks and weirdness are much more obvious than they really are, this is called the 'Spotlight effect'). Always remember, tiny changes will feel huge to you, while remaining imperceptible to others. The more you can alter your behaviour, the more situations you can control, and the more influential you will become.

Hopefully, you have also found a few techniques in this section about which you thought 'Oh yeah, I already do that anyway', or have read it before. It's not surprising, these techniques are common *because they work*. Seek out more opportunities where you can sneakily slip these methods into ordinary conversations, presentations and negotiations. Notice how they work, and perhaps devise a few of your own.

The Style

Part Three

We are nearing the end of this journey, my friend. By now you should have found a variety of ways to significantly alter the way you present yourself to the world, and be regularly taking opportunities to test things out. In The Style, we'll focus on putting you back into what you're doing. We'll focus on reading your audience to become highly attuned to the behaviour and emotional states of those around you. We'll talk a bit about vulnerability, and how it endears us to others.

Then we'll get to what is, for me, the whole point of this book: using your skills to improve the lives of others, by endowing them with skills and challenging them with humour. It's a method of coaching I learned and loved so much, I've turned it into a way for being, for life. When I learned of it, it was called Provocative Therapy. I call it Provocative Style.

I will then challenge you to sustain your momentum by teaching these skills to others. It will test everything you've learned so far and ensure that you continue to learn. I'll ask you to define your purpose in life, to decide what you stand for, and to present your values in a way that recruits people to your cause. It might sound grand, but if you don't feel ready, by then, you will be.

In this part we'll cover the following elements.

→ How to read people, their eyes, body language and patterns.
→ How to build relationships with touch.
→ The importance of vulnerability and admitting mistakes.
→ How to use humour to defuse situations.
→ Methods to challenge undesirable behaviour from others.
→ The rules of engagement – setting boundaries with people around you.
→ Teaching skills to others.
→ Defining your values.
→ Creating a purpose for yourself.

Reading your audience

To be effective as a communicator, leader, influencer, provocateur, or indeed as any kind of human, it's important to remain vigilantly aware of those around you. We give off signals all the time, about what we like, what scares us, and what excites or confuses us (though confusion seems to be the only one we display deliberately). Our body language speaks volumes. We're constantly spewing out clues about what will motivate us to shift our opinion. To benefit from that rich deluge of data, you must remain alert and attuned to the people around you. You'll spot interesting social dynamics, develop an eye for deception, and be able to structure and target your messages with precision and compassion.

For all of the patterns and quirks of behaviour that you see: **it means what it is**. Hunching and mumbling does not 'mean' shy, even though it usually does. Those simplistic answers cloud our perception by clogging the mind with certainty. Try to remain filled with doubt and curiosity. Although less certain, you'll have a much more useful picture of the world.

It's in the eyes

The eyes are the window to our consciousness. We think about what we're looking at, and we look at what we're thinking about. The eyes tell us a lot, which is why evolution has devoted so much cognitive architecture to allow us to read the eyes (and therefore intentions) of others. If you want to know who someone fancies, watch who they watch when their eye begins to wander. If you want to know who's leading a group, be aware of where everyone looks when the conversation grinds to a halt. When people are interested in your story, they'll watch you, or let their eyes defocus as they watch the pictures you're painting in their mind. If they're not interested, they'll be looking at their phone, willing it to ring them with news of a family emergency (it's amazing how much carnage we wish upon our nearest and dearest when we're trapped listening to a boring tale).

Eye contact is hard-wired by evolution to communicate confidence, aggression and interest. In order to get noticed, be listened to and believed, you must practise holding eye contact for longer. It's hard to hold eye contact. We have evolved in such a way that as eye contact is maintained (particularly with a stranger) our pulse skyrockets and we're flooded with adrenaline. Some call this the 'fuck or fight' limit because after three seconds, you're likely going to end up doing one of them.

Hold it longer. The more you do it, the easier it gets.

Do this:
Have a heavy eye contact day

Set yourself a challenge to become better at holding eye contact, for life. At first, start off with a single day. During this day, make time to be among people you know and people you don't, perhaps taking a long walk through the streets at lunchtime.

Set yourself the challenge of making eye contact with people, and letting them be the one to break it. Yes, it will be weird, that's the idea – you want to experience feeling that rush, and more importantly, experience what it's like overruling the desire to look away.

If you want to make the eye contact flirty, or at least non-threatening, smile. Notice that smiling before you hold eye contact seems like you're already happy, or perhaps a bit weird. Smiling after establishing eye contact is a sign of approval. It's much nicer to that person. Try both and notice the results.

Unconscious body language

Without noticing, we'll often give away a lot about what we're feeling and thinking with our body language. People will nod when they agree with someone, often without noticing it (and nodding while saying no is sometimes an indication of deception). This is called the 'ideomotor effect', in which ideas will cause small, or sometimes quite large involuntary (or perhaps more accurately, unconscious) muscle movements, in line with the thought we're holding (hence idea-motor). This effect is what makes Ouija boards work, which claim to contact dead spirits asking them to spell out words on a board, with a group of people holding a glass or some other device. Everyone in the group is pushing the glass around with their thoughts, while remaining certain that they aren't.

Look out for the following body language

→ **Face the leader:** people often face the dominant person in the group squarely with their shoulders.

→ **Feet signal desire:** we point our feet towards what we want or where we want to go, be that a person, the buffet or the door.

→ **Tense breath:** people often hold their breath when they're tense.

→ **Open gestures are dominant:** broad, open gestures suggest dominance, that someone doesn't feel threatened, as will exposing the throat by lifting the chin.

→ **Closed gestures are submission:** downcast eyes, a small voice and gestures which cover the chest, face and groin signal submission, like a dog tucking in its tail.

→ **Resistance to speak:** covering the mouth or retreating while talking signals our desire to distance ourselves from what we're saying, and is sometimes considered a symptom of deception.

→ **Tapping and giggling away the energy:** tapping is often caused by an excess of energy, perhaps from a highly energised or nervous person, as is giggling. Notice when it starts, or more interestingly, when it stops.

→ **Flushing an adrenal load:** flushing is a sign that someone has experienced a dump of adrenaline, often from embarrassment, but sometimes because a topic or person has them worried or aroused.

→ **Dilated pupils:** pupil dilation again signals arousal, either through fear or excitement. I've heard this a lot but despite watching people closely, I've never noticed someone's pupils dilate.

Watching for a change

Keep an eye out for deviations from normal behaviour. This can be easy to do with friends and family members. To spot changes in people you've just met, you must first calibrate their normal state, letting them relax and getting a feel for that state. Then you can test them with the listing method which follows, or watch them experience changes in their environment, keeping an eye out for moments of uncharacteristic excitement or unpredictable anger, a sudden stillness during conversation, or nervous twitching and covering of the mouth. Giggles, sudden fascination with one's shoes... these are all hints.

Listing method to spot odd reactions

Watching for a change is particularly effective for feeling out topics that people won't bring up themselves. Sometimes it'll be something they want to keep secret, want to talk about but believe they aren't allowed to, or don't yet feel they have the courage to raise. A useful technique is to run ideas past someone, like plates of fish on a sushi train, keeping an eye out for what piques their interest or evokes some sort of reaction.

When you ask directly 'Is it X?', you're reading their reaction to you *thinking* this was what was bothering them. When you list the possibilities casually, as if running ideas past them, they will be less guarded in their responses and respond to how each one feels to them. The more noticeable the change, the more they are willing you to notice it (at least subconsciously). It's often our way of telling the truth when we don't want to be seen or heard saying it.

- ✗ **Don't ask directly:** 'Is it money? Is it your role?'
- ✔ **Do listing. Keep it relaxed, almost as if you're talking to yourself:** 'I guess I might feel I deserve more money, respect, responsibility, time off...'
- ✔ **Do finish your list with a crazy suggestion:** '...it could be the terrible instant coffee, or perhaps you just want to punch Ken in the throat and fill his car with cement.'

Making a silly suggestion at the end will allow them to laugh it off and return to a happy state, having avoided the inquisition they may have been expecting (though nobody really expects an inquisition). After noting the change, you might not need to probe further. The positive feeling that comes with laughing, and your deliberate retreat from the topic will leave them feeling closer to you and safer in your company, and thus more inclined to tell you what was going on. There is serious value in not taking things too seriously.

Noticing people's patterns

People often have fantastically recursive and fractal patterns in their lives, such that tiny habits reinforce themselves, and are often miniature manifestations of much larger personality traits. People who struggle to choose what they want from the menu and continually change their order often replicate that pattern when choosing lovers, careers, or what to wear. People who complain about being interrupted often interrupt people to say so, and people who think that others are 'out to get them' are often quite vindictive to others, and frame it to themselves as a kind of proactive defence. Watch for patterns of behaviour, within yourself and the people around you.

Useful patterns may exist, like breathing and getting up for work in the morning, but we won't focus on them here. All patterns start out as a simple behaviour with a good intent (conscious or otherwise), but as they become more automatic, they become less effective, and are expressing themselves in contexts which are inappropriate. Varied behaviour is much more powerful than patterns.

Examples of behavioural patterns

→ **'No...'** – some people habitually rejoin conversations with the phrase 'No'. Perhaps you are one of them. If you are: No. That's naughty. Say 'yes' more often.

→ **'Yeah, but...'** – people sometimes see it as their role to find flaws in an idea, or search for exceptions. Yeah, it can be helpful, but only in small doses.

→ **'You decide'** and **'What do you think?'** – some people persistently defer to others, preferring never to make decisions themselves. It's often interwoven with seeking out reassurance and excessively agreeing with people to be 'nice'.

→ **Speaking last** – often a symptom of a larger issue – of not taking or not making opportunities for themselves.

→ **'This is probably stupid, but...'** or **'This isn't fully ready yet...'** – people who trash their own ideas before they've even presented anything. Upon hearing it we don't think 'Well this is a work in progress and they have high standards', we think 'So why are you showing it to us?'. Instead of saying 'This isn't ready yet' say 'I'd love your feedback on this, as I'm still developing it.'

→ **'I know'** or **'Yeah...'** when it sounds like **'No'** – we often use this to let someone know that we think they're right in their advice to us, and that we already know they're right, but it comes across as the opposite. Try saying 'Yes, you're right', 'Good point' or 'I agree'. If you're agreeing, *sound* like you're agreeing!

→ **'Coupled' behaviour** – this is where certain stimuli result in the same reaction, such as covering the mouth each time they say a certain person's name, giggling when being flirted with, or getting abusive while drunk.

Do this:

Spot and challenge a pattern

Notice a few people around you and how they may fall prey to some of these patterns. Go through the list and note anyone who follows these patterns. Come up with some of your own from the behaviour you see around you.

Try these two ways of challenging people around you to adjust these patterns. Have a go, it can be quite tricky!

→ Point it out. Be kind and speak rationally about it, workshop with them reasons why and how it could stop.

→ Next, laugh at it. Suggest that it's a great habit to have and lay out some reasons to continue, or perhaps suggest that they might not have the ability to stop.

You'll probably notice that being kind and rational feels 'nice' but that it is much less effective than jokingly being 'mean'. Why is that?

Turn your eye inward: look over the list, particularly including the patterns you came up with. Do you fall prey to any of these?

Broken thinking patterns

There are certain flaws in our thinking that cause us to hold unhelpful beliefs about the world around us. They occur when we fall prey to our cognitive biases discussed in The Words. These broken thinking patterns display themselves in a variety of ways, and are often detrimental to our happiness. Listen for them, in your own speech and in the words of others. In a bit we'll discuss Provocative ways to challenge these patterns. For now, just notice them:

→ **Getting offended:** we choose what offends us, though we don't usually see it that way. We erect barriers around beliefs which are fragile or ideas that make us uncomfortable (which explains why a significant portion of men who self-identify as opposed to homosexuality get aroused by homosexual imagery). Claiming offence gives power to the offence-taker, often allowing them to dictate the behaviour of others. For these reasons, finding things to be offended by becomes a bit addictive. The problem is claiming that we're offended by something will ensure two things: that we really are upset by it, and people will use it to upset us.

→ **'I've tried *everything*!':** asking for advice and arguing with it, or perpetually asking for it but never following it. Nobody, ever, anywhere, has tried *everything*. These phrases are used to control a discussion and elicit guilt and sympathy from others.

→ **Finding fault in the world** and looking for things that don't work and complaining about them. The world is plenty broken. Due to the long, healthy, safe lives we lead, we've been afforded lots of spare time to look for the breakages. This habit is common among activist types, who continually point out inequality or other perceived evils, particularly in systems which are quite organic (such as corporations making profit by paying workers less and using cheap materials). It's much more effective to be happy, accept the world as it is now, and use that happiness and understanding to influence the future.

→ **'I'm terrible at...':** when we say negative things about ourselves, we are bound by a social contract to continually prove that we were right. What started as humility becomes real disability, just ask anyone who says 'I can't do accents' or 'tell jokes' or 'sing'.

→ **'Knowing my luck...':** consistently expecting the worst to happen will ensure the worst will happen, a claim well supported by behavioural research.

Speak for Yourself

→ **Wound collecting:** similar to offence taking, this is a term coined by body language expert Joe Navarro. It's the habit of collecting perceived slights against oneself, which are remembered and nurtured and combine to form an imagined conspiracy. Wound collectors sometimes act in a way that perpetuates the problem (by starting arguments or missing deadlines) to trigger a predictable negative response, like being shouted at or losing a contract, so they can feel vindicated: 'I *knew* it!'

→ **Generalisations:** 'He *always* does that'. Really, always? Even while he's asleep?

→ **Assumptions:** 'She's trying to upset me' or 'When he says X, he really means Y.' An assumption is any conclusion about someone else's intent that is not apparent in their behaviour. We often fall into these brain black holes when we sit alone and try to reason through someone else's behaviour, without gathering any new data that would challenge our assumptions. The brain doesn't like being alone and will punish us by seeking out and investing in the worst of all possible meanings. The simplest test for this is to ask them (or yourself): how would that person explain their behaviour?

→ **Moral absolutes:** the words 'should', 'must', 'ought to', 'have to' or any appeal to unnamed absolute moral values. 'They shouldn't do that' is a useless statement and a barrier to empathic thought. Every time you hear the word 'should', you're hearing someone's brain die a little bit. Clearly, whoever's doing that, thinks they *should*, or at the very least, that they *can*. Delete the word 'should' from your vocabulary.

The only exception to using 'should' is with an IF/THEN condition, when the desired outcome is stated and logically valid, such as 'If you want to get a raise, you should ask for one' or 'If you want to sell more phones, you should do some marketing' or 'If you want to get a girl, you should probably shave off that beard' (the same goes if you want to get a guy).

Try to treat the word 'should' the way Indians do. In spoken Hindi, 'should' is almost indistinguishable from the word 'want'. The sentence 'They should label these things properly' sounds exactly the same as 'I would like them to label these things properly.' This is quite a consciousness-raising idea, which once embraced, is very effective at turning arguments into discussions.

→ **It can't be done:** it's common for people to assert something can't be done because they've already tried. They *want* it to be impossible because otherwise it will reflect poorly upon them as having failed. Their desire to see themselves as capable will motivate their reasoning: 'Oh don't ask him. I already asked, he said no.' Remember, 99 no's and one yes is still a yes.

It should go without saying, but these symptoms of brain-death and patterned behaviours aren't always bad, and don't always need to be pointed out to the sufferer. There can be a temptation to weaponise these tools for personal development. You might recall a time when a workmate, friend or partner came back from some course with a new arsenal of terms to describe your self-destructive behaviour. In most cases, if people are lacking the common ground (of having read the book or gone on the course), it will cause an adverse response.

Obviously, none of these lists are exhaustive. Lists of habits, laws, or types of people and ways to deal with them are innumerable and can be found all over the place. They're easy to invent, and I don't think they're very useful. I have no interest in codifying people's behaviour or lumping us into different categories and I encourage you to actively resist the urge. Instead, I encourage you to keep an open mind, spot patterns, develop hypotheses, and invent challenges of your own.

It's important to test these ideas. Actively seek to find the exception to any rule, because that's often the clue to helping someone break free. For example, people who self-identify as 'shy' often become quite outspoken if you insensitively tell them to 'Just stop being shy', or say something demonstrably wrong about a subject they know and care a lot about.

Do this:

Challenge your own thinking

Spotting flaws in others is easy, spotting flaws in our own thinking, and changing it, now that is a real challenge. Remain vigilant against these symptoms of broken thinking, and when you find yourself indulging in them (we all do), challenge them. If you hear yourself saying 'should', rephrase it and say 'I'd like', or 'This may work better' or try asking a question.

▶

You may notice other patterns, of avoiding opportunities or getting upset easily. Find ways to challenge these. Instead of focusing on 'not' doing them, focus on what else you could do in that moment, or methods to avoid things that trigger these patterned responses.

The Provocative Style

Chapter Eleven

There are times in our lives when a certain idea, a book, a moment, will change us forever. Mine came when I was first introduced to the remarkable work of Frank Farrelly, and a style of psychotherapy he'd invented called Provocative Therapy. His work involved offering honest feedback to people in short, rambling and profanity-filled sessions. He'd play the devil's advocate, encouraging them to laugh at their problems. He believed in using humour as a tool for change. Frank was a loveable and cranky old man (at least when I met him), who developed Provocative Therapy as a method for dealing with people who have been labelled as psychologically disturbed. It is quite strange to be writing about him now, as he died only last year. We all die. You will too. Frank was particularly keen on talking to people about death because it offers a sudden perspective.

We all laugh, too, and it must be for a very, very good reason. Dunno what it is. I know it must be a good reason because evolution doesn't instil a sense of humour in every human being on the planet *by accident*. Have you ever experienced one of those magical moments when you're standing on the street, see something quite strange, and you laugh in time with a stranger? Don't you feel bonded with them, and permitted, perhaps even *obliged*, to talk to them? There is something about laughter that connects us. We know there is something potent and inherently positive about laughter. We say 'Laughter is the best medicine', but we say that as if it's a herb that we don't know how to inject, inhale, or wrap in plastic and sell to one another, *yet*. We know that people who laugh loudly and frequently make better lovers, friends, bosses and planet-mates. Laughter is a powerful, wonderful, and thoroughly bizarre phenomenon. Until I discovered Frank's work, I'd never found a way to *use* laughter for a purpose.

Thinking about problems leads us to feeling bad, which becomes easier to do once we've done it a lot of times. It gets abbreviated, like arguments you see a married couple have, when their shorthand insults become so short, onlookers have no idea why one of them suddenly starts shouting. We all have patterns for thinking we're stupid, fat, lazy or procrastinate too much. Money problems, love life problems, health issues, challenges at work, family issues, existential crises and 'what am I doing with my life' moments plague us all. The more we think about them and feel down, the stronger and faster that neural superhighway becomes. We cannot ignore them, nor can we benignly 'choose' to feel differently about them. Further bad feelings will follow. Unless...

You laugh. When you laugh, the highways to sadness are torn up by physical and mental convulsions of happiness. When that unhappy idea next travels down the highway, new tracks have been laid which lead off to a memory of laughter and togetherness.

This is the fundamental belief behind Provocative Style, which I believe to be testable and falsifiable: *if we laugh while we think about a problem, the laughter changes our current and future emotional responses to that thought.*

By making people laugh about their problems, you're fixing their lives. Humour offers perspective and confidence, an ability and a desire to improve the lives of those around you. This makes humour an incredibly powerful tool for leadership.

Humour and leadership

There is a link between leadership and humour that is easily recognised by those who know leadership. In a survey by Accountemps, 79 per cent of chief financial officers interviewed considered a sense of humour to be 'somewhat' or 'very' important for new employees. Comedy writer Mel Helitzer writes:

> 'Fortune Magazine queried human resource directors of Fortune 500 companies as to what qualifications they looked for in middle management executives, the top three answers were (1) knowledge of the product; (2) respect for the bottom line; and (3) a sense of humour.'

You'll note that there is no mention of leadership experience or ability, and this is for *management executives*! It's as if humour, to them, already indicates leadership.

The Royal Marines' four core values are courage, determination, unselfishness, and (perhaps quite surprisingly), 'cheerfulness in the face of adversity', which they also call 'Commando Humour'. I shit you not:

> 'The 40 Commando's [Manoeuvre Support Group] *emphasized the importance of humour to the conduct of their mission. Indeed, in recalling the event, it was not the memory [of] fear which was paramount in the members of this group's minds but the memory*

*of funny incidents; troops falling into mud while debussing from
Chinooks at the Manifold Metering Station or simply the look on
comrades' faces at certain points in the operation. During the
ambush near Abu Al Khasib, a team member in the leading vehicle
was amused by the fact that the Iraqi gunman who had opened fire
could have missed his colleague's oversized head – so big was the
target presented to him.'*

Dr Anthony King (Department Of Sociology,
University of Exeter, May 2004, *The Ethos Of
The Royal Marines, The Precise Application Of Will*)

The Royal Marines have levels of post-traumatic stress disorder which
are almost equivalent to the general public, who aren't regularly shot at
and blown up (3.8 per cent versus 3 per cent). It appears that humour,
in allowing marines to find the lighter side of dire situations, changes
their memory of them. It offers a way to bond and laugh about difficult
times shared. This describes humour's most valuable leadership
quality: to bind people not just to us, and our cause, but to other
people within the cause.

The laws of leadership and humour

Try new things. Anyone who can recognise funny, can be funny,
it's simply a matter of trying new things. Keep trying until you strike
something unexpected and new. Great leaders and innovators are
leading *because* they are willing to test the bounds of social conformity,
and seek out new opportunities. That takes...

Courage. Humour can be learned, but unfunny people rarely learn to
become funny because it takes so much courage. Humour, like sales,
like dating, like being an entrepreneur, takes getting up one time more
than you got knocked down. The courage to continually put your hand to
things that might fail aptly describes the gulf between the good and the
great, the unfunny and the funny, the hard-working and the successful.

Remain open to feedback, and focus on what works. Be
aware of your audience. Acknowledge failure, and soak up those times
it all comes together beautifully. Take the feedback, accept it. Define
yourself with your successes. Learn from (or reframe) your failures, and
move on, again, to try something new.

Timing is key. Knowing when to push a client to close a deal takes the same kind of intuition to time the delivery of a punchline; too soon and they aren't hungry for it, too late and they've forgotten about it and moved on. It's important to know when to crack a joke about a recent celebrity death, just as it's important to pick when to broach the topic of promotion with your boss. Most of all, it takes presence of mind to persist in a state of permanent preparedness, and speak up or step in at a moment's notice. If it needs to be said, then say it, now. Don't be that person who thinks of something relevant or funny, says nothing, and gets grumpy with themselves when someone else says it. Definitely don't be the person who leaves the meeting and sends a well-worded email to everyone explaining why that thing we all agreed to do is actually not such a good idea. We hate that person. We hate their idea. Particularly if it's right. Make your moment, step up, and open your bloody mouth.

Be willing to push boundaries. The greatest innovations are totally unexpected, and initially most are met with ridicule. Do the unexpected, be willing to offend people. Things get a lot funnier when we know we shouldn't laugh. Don't go around intentionally offending people, but don't sit neatly inside the rules of social propriety either, avoiding making a mark lest someone gets cranky. Rules are there to stop people being bad, but they also limit us from being great. Be aware of people's boundaries, push at them, toy with them, and violate them pleasantly. In doing so, you're encouraging others to become emotionally resilient, making them more functional human beings.

Knowledge and awareness. Humour requires knowledge of content, in recognising similarity in dissimilar circumstances, in seeing and delighting in incongruity, and knowing your audience. In business, you need the same thing – knowledge of your product, of the market and gaps within it, of your workmates and your clients. The better you are at inspiring useful emotions in them, the more successful you will be.

Recognise opportunity in crisis. Whenever things are going really badly wrong, there is something funny happening. It's often said that comedy is tragedy plus time, and the sooner you can start laughing, the better. Just as a comedian can rescue a routine by acknowledging a bad joke, an astute trader can recognise a tanking market and invest in gold. I was working on a film in India in my first main role and the film went belly-up in spectacular style, with explosions, dead horses and all sorts of drama. My father told me that 'a disaster is an adventure misconstrued' and in time, it became clear that he was right. Writing about that experience led, in a rather circuitous fashion, to me writing this book. Next time something is going colossally wrong, keep your chin up and your mind focused on outcomes because when the dust settles, it's the person who kept their cool that will end up on top.

Build relationships with in-jokes

Our fondest friends are those with whom we share many happy memories. When something funny happens among friends, we'll often develop a shorthand way of saying it, perhaps a gesture, a word, or more often a phrase. Each time it recurs, the pleasant feeling returns, and we build new memories of fun times.

With your friends, in your workplace or anywhere, seek out and nurture funny moments. When someone says something original and spontaneous, repeat it. Appreciate and reward them for bringing a bit of novelty into your life. When someone starts using a new term for something, use it with them. You may develop your own private language that becomes so damn enjoyable, you might be inclined to do it in front of others, to their exclusion. Thankfully, you're highly aware of your audience, and much better behaved than that.

It's probably worthwhile noting that this is true of all jargons and lingos: they often make the speakers feel good, accepted, and are a simpler way of describing recurring ideas and technical concepts that plain English can't handle. They can also serve to exclude and de-personalise things, so be mindful of that.

Revitalise the joke and make it new. Make new ones, with new people who are included, so that it becomes funny and spreads like a virus, infecting people with a sense of belonging.

How to build in-jokes

→ Give things names and characters: that guy with crazy hair at the coffee shop can be called Einstein, and his coffee machine is a particle accelerator.

→ When people misspeak, accept it: 'Estabrish' could be a refreshing new soft drink.

→ Bond with old friends in new environments. Go bowling with workmates. Work with your bowling buddies. The more contexts in which we know someone, the more 'sides' of them we see, and the more we like them.

Sales humour

In sales there is an unspoken tension that develops between salesperson and buyer that arises as a function of the roles; the buyer knows they're being persuaded, which is in direct conflict with their illusion of autonomy. Anything that suggests to them that they are a puppet of fate, or susceptible to influence, will cause an adverse reaction (which is why everyone says 'advertising doesn't work on me' while slurping down a can of cola). To relieve this tension, you can lampoon your 'role' as salesperson. When selling weddings, I used to run a great double act with the boss. He was separated from his wife, which gave us great material to crack jokes about dysfunctional marriages. Couples were used to (and I suspect, tired of) salesmen who talked as if we live in a sickly sweet fairy tale with true love lasting forever, and weddings being the most special day of their lives. It insulted the customer's intelligence (who knew we did this for a living and were merely paying lip service to these illusions), and built an awkward paradigm in which we all had to maintain an improbable lie. It's a bit like pretending you still believe in Santa Claus when you're around children. Once the child sees through it, pretending Santa exists will only serve to undermine their trust. Instead, the boss and I would crack jokes about second weddings being half price, which engaged couples invariably found hilarious (remember that biases cause people to see their marriage as lasting forever while knowing that statistically, most won't). It would mock our position, breaking that tension, and show us as fallible. They laughed and felt comfortable with us, meaning they'd see us as honest, and worth trusting with the first most special day of their lives.

I used to enjoy telling potential customers a story about when I called the home number of someone who'd made an enquiry on the website, and a grandmother picked up the phone. Granny didn't speak English, so I started speaking in my questionable Hindi. I meant to ask her 'Have you enquired about having a wedding?' but I'm a bit iffy with sentence construction and don't know the word 'enquiry', so I actually asked 'Would you like to get married?' The shocked old Indian grandmother responded 'Nahin! Mai shaadi ho gayi hai' (No! I'm already married), but I ploughed on, asking 'Well does anyone else round there want to get married?' To young British-Indian couples (who can easily imagine the scandalised granny, they probably live with three or four of them), it was a funny story of a bumbling foreigner who appeared to be shopping around for brides. It helped sell weddings because it was self-deprecating and it tackled the perception of me as a white salesman who spoke Hindi being 'too slick'. It also makes for a useful example of using vulnerability (and the right amount of self-deprecation) to endear yourself to a client. The 'pratfall effect' is a well-tested phenomenon which describes how making a mistake will make you more likable, but *only if you're in danger of being 'too perfect'*. It's important to avoid joking about the product or service you offer being inferior, just as I was not joking about ruining weddings (though I would sometimes joke about 'accidentally' asking out the bride's sister, which is particularly funny if she's in the room and not at all interested).

- ✘ **Don't employ humour about the customer's haggling (nobody believes it):** 'You're too good at this negotiating stuff, I'll be sleeping rough if I make many more deals like this.'
- ✔ **Do employ humour about their haggling (compliments are nice):** 'You're great at this negotiating stuff. Perhaps *you* should be selling *me* the holiday' (gets funnier when you let them sell it back to you, and start asking them questions about stuff they haven't asked).

Using humour to defuse a situation

When people start getting aggressive, thinking of funny things to say can be difficult, but it's bloody effective. In situations where backing down might be seen as accepting defeat, and stepping up might just escalate things, humour, if well pitched, can often flip the situation.

Speak for Yourself

If you're a beginner...

The safest option is to use self-deprecating humour to defuse tense situations. A friend of mine was in a bar and bumped some thug in a crowd, who spilled their drink on him. The thug was about to turn ugly. My friend made a joke about how he loved having big nights out, but preferred to wet his own pants. Even though the thug didn't find it very funny, it got attention and laughter from everyone around them. The humour brought people on side, whose laughter would have sounded like a pack of barking dogs to the thug. The joke was also self-deprecating, reducing the thug's desire to fight. He made some gruff comment and went on his way. When you can laugh *with* someone who's angry, it's even more effective. It's quite safe to make jokes about something totally removed from the situation, about trains running late, politicians lying, or if you're British, continuing to complain about the weather, just make it funny.

If you're intermediate...

If you're about to get told off, try saying something silly or strange right as the discussion starts. 'Is this tie on straight? It feels like a noose.' If you share a history, you can 'suddenly remind' them of a fun time you had together (see in-jokes). They're preparing for a difficult conversation and are running over your past misdeeds to validate, for themselves, the need to tell you off (so they can retain the 'I'm a good person' feeling). Interrupt that thought process. Make them feel good, then take the lead, returning to 'get down to it': 'I think you wanted to talk about me coming in late.' It shows that you weren't running away from the issue. If you're going to get a talking-to from a boss or a lover, you're going to get a talking to. They'll respect you for that, and they'll be in a good mood, relieved they didn't have to restart the ugly discussion. They'll no longer want to make you feel bad (which we only do if we're upset), they'll just want you to realise how you made them feel, or accept that what you did was a little bit naughty. That's fine. We all make mistakes.

If you're an expert...

A more dangerous (and therefore exciting) method is to crack a joke at the expense of whoever's escalating the tension, *about* them escalating the tension. I was running an event and some confusion about what time it ended had resulted in a mixed message being sent to the organiser to shut it down two hours early. He flew into a rage, marched up to me, and started shouting at me in front of his guests, threatening to have me fired and the venue shut down (considering I worked at the venue, these seemed like mutually exclusive threats, but whatever). I tried to match him and lead him down a calmer state, and serenely pointed out that as nothing had actually been turned off, the booze was still flowing, the music was still playing, and none of the guests had been bothered. He was not convinced. 'You've made me look a fool in front of my guests!' he asserted. Abandoning the gentler techniques, I grinned at him and retorted: 'To be fair, I think you're doing a pretty good job of that yourself.' The people within earshot chuckled, he smirked, and to my surprise he said 'Yes, perhaps you're right.' The humour had defused the tension, and his ability to laugh (essentially at himself) had let him re-establish his maturity in front of his guests. Without that, I'd have lost a valuable client and he'd have looked like a hot-head.

Be funny, but don't be a joke

There is something very different between telling jokes and having a good sense of humour. A good sense of humour will see the similarity in dissimilar circumstances, be perceptive and tuned in to those around them, and sit in situations that might be quite dire, and have the timing and confidence to expose the lighter side. Cracking jokes is simply a task of memorising someone else's wit and regurgitating it on cue for dutiful ripples of tired laughter, like a trained dolphin does predictable tricks for cold dead fish. It can be entertaining, but it's also a little bit sad.

Pick your moments to be funny and be willing to engage seriously, and keep your humour relevant and about what's happening in the moment.

Build stronger relationships through touch

Pay keen attention to how much and what kind of physical contact you share with people. Sometimes a playful (gentle!) punch in the arm or nudge in the ribs can soften a message and change its entire tone. Be aware of your proximity and level of contact with people, using touch to soften harsh messages (which we'll talk about in a moment) or suggest that they be taken as a joke. With a touch on the arm you say 'I'm here with you.'

This is particularly important when dealing with difficult issues or giving feedback which might be taken badly – just be careful you don't use contact to incentivise and reinforce negative states (parents who hug their child every time it cries soon find the child cries all the time).

Sit or stand side by side (rather than face to face)

We think about what we're looking at. When we look at other people, we think about what they're thinking. This makes face to face discussions more adversarial, and can cause them to turn towards fights because we're trying to figure out what the other person wants from the situation. When you're side by side, your conversation partner is free to look at other things and stay in their own head with their thoughts, while dealing with a problem that's 'out there', in front of you both.

Walking with someone is even more powerful, particularly if it's somewhere calming and natural. Parks are great for problem-solving discussions. Trees, greenery and water tell our primitive brain to chill out, and the locomotion limits recursive discussion, pushing the conversation forwards, towards solutions.

Physical contact

Be aware of *when* and *how* you touch people. Physical contact signals acceptance, and if people let you, they will immediately start feeling closer to you. If they don't want you to touch them, they'll tense or recoil a bit, even if they try to stop themselves. Be aware of this. Continuing to touch someone when they don't want to be touched will quickly make them feel icky around you. Touching them while they're laughing and feeling good about themselves will associate those feelings with that touch, and they'll start to like you. A lot.

For Provocative discussions, physical contact is an absolute must. If you gently poke at someone, pat them, nudge them or lean against them, you can say almost anything you want. With that touch, your body is signalling to them your positive intent while your words may be saying the exact opposite. This is one of the most important parts of the incongruence in Provocative. Touch people as you're delivering the harshest part of your message, and they'll hear it with the good humour and love with which it was intended.

Calibrate and respect people's boundaries

Different people have different boundaries. Most of us feel comfortable with a fleeting pat on the back of the forearm or hand. Some people enjoy someone touching the small of their back, others don't. People with six-packs won't mind you touching their stomach, but chubbers often will. Generally, avoid iffy areas, and engage in about as much contact with people as they do with you. If they pat your knee, that's permission to pat theirs. The general gist: be constantly establishing boundaries, and violating them, pleasantly.

Maintain a close physical proximity

Proximity speaks of emotional closeness, so if you relax people while being close to them, they will feel quite close with you. When having conversations, try to stay at the same level as them – avoid talking down at someone while you're standing and they're sitting. If they're shorter than you, lean on a desk.

Some people will metaphorically and physically retreat from certain topics. In Provocative discussions, those are exactly the topics you want to address. Try copying Frank's method of sternly and lovingly communicating 'Don't run away. Stay here with me.'

Stepping out of your comfort zone

Now we're getting towards the more sticky end of matters – where I'll start to suggest things which might cause some of you to think I've gone nuts.

While working in a horrendously dull office job, I was sat near a man who would regale us each morning with his various complaints, usually about his health, sometimes about the 'system' or the 'unfairness of it all'. I got bored of it and interrupted him one day to say 'Don't worry. You'll be dead soon', the inflection suggested that I was going to say 'and none of that will bother you any more' but I said: 'and we won't have to listen to your moaning any more.' We all laughed. He didn't, but he did stop whining in public. That's an example of a quite direct and harsh intervention. Frank has examples of even harsher ones. You can relax – I won't ask you to go quite that far, though I do invite you to try it out once or twice. Although it can be effective, it's not for everyone. It takes empathy, skill and experience to ensure those kind of comments don't get you fired and still have the desired effect.

In many cases, gentler approaches can still work wonders. I was coaching a guy who was managing a team of people, one of whom continually complained that her career wasn't progressing as fast as she'd like. It was annoying him and those around him, but it wasn't really disciplinary-worthy behaviour (it's absurd if you think about it, we let problems get worse, just so that we can deal with them!). When we next met, he informed me he'd taken a Provocative approach with her. When she was again complaining about her career, he said 'I know how you can get promoted!' A hush surrounded them, as everyone expected to hear some sage advice. He finished: 'You should complain more.' Everyone laughed, as did she. The laughter of those around her sent a message that it had been annoying them too (otherwise they wouldn't have found the 'advice' funny). The humour made it easier to say, and much more effective than a serious chat, and it broke the pattern – and *that* is the point. When people get in a patterned behaviour, they're so experienced at it, they often do it on autopilot. They're not thinking 'How does this sound to others?' or 'Is this getting me what I want?', they're just doing it because it's what they do. Humour is the perfect way to interrupt this behaviour, disrupt that wiring, and force them to observe their own behaviour, as if through a funhouse mirror. When we next talked about the complainer, I was informed she had abandoned complaining in favour of being more pragmatic – she was now focused on getting what she wanted, rather than complaining about not having it.

Rather than saying 'You can do it' and have someone enumerate the obstacles they face, a Provocative motivator might suggest that they can't, and point out those obstacles themselves. A Provocative boss might present her ambitious but shy employee with a world in which he never puts his hand up, never takes initiative, and lives out the rest of his professional life in the same, unfulfilling role (you'll be astounded by how much people laugh at an image of themselves, at 70, still working in a junior role, complete with hearing loss and occasional incontinence). The job of a Provocateur is to find the moments, and the courage, to speak aloud people's darkest fears and most self-destructive thoughts, to play the devil's advocate, but with the skill and awareness to do it with love and humour. When it's done cleverly, with feigned seriousness, a nudge and a smile, you'll enjoy it. We love talking positively about ourselves, we just need to be justified in doing so.

Have an obvious, positive intent, and you'll find that people are far more resilient than you first expect. Whenever I'm teaching Provocative Style, particularly to other coaches, they often say 'But you can't say that to someone who's really upset or insecure, you'd only say that to a confident person' but I disagree. Confident people are well accustomed to getting the piss taken out of them. It's a by-product of being confident and as such, publicly cracking jokes at someone's expense, when done well, reinforces their confidence. Shy people often miss out on that, and many get suspicious that it happens in their absence. In my experience, the most upset and insecure people respond best to a public lampooning, provided they're given an opportunity to retort, *and they take it.*

Provocative is definitely not about being horrible to people. It's the opposite. It should free you, to be fully you, and exercise a fuller range of behaviour. That includes being quiet and contemplative, kind and listening, asking questions, yet being forceful, funny and persuasive when necessary. Remember the story of being told by a drunk stranger that I had a terrible posture? It was indelicate, and by the bounds of social acceptability it was rude, but it worked. Sometimes, harsh comments are exactly the ones we need to hear. It's a terrible shame that we only hear these thoughts from lovers and friends in times of anger. I implore you to find ways to speak these necessary truths, and tell them with the love of a friend, the style of a comic, and the harshness of a drunken stranger.

A word of warning

Be mindful of employment laws, and be careful about what you say. If you say to someone 'You are worthless' and your intent is to provoke an assertive state in them, remember that 'I was being Provocative' will be difficult to explain at an employment tribunal. I'm certainly not going to take the stand on your behalf. Jest is poorly conveyed when set in print and recited by gormless lawyers. Using these methods requires a bit of courage and a lot of awareness.

A point also needs to be made about ethics. Even behaviour that doesn't fall foul of employment law needs to be addressed. Deliberately and humorously putting someone down is not being Provocative, it's just mean. This kind of behaviour does not go unnoticed by others and will cause a deep rot in the soul. The only way to lead people, improve your life, and be happy, is to seek to uplift those around you. Provocative Style comes from a place of love and seeks the betterment of everyone who experiences it, even those who merely witness it.

It takes a keen insight and a bit of experimentation to find out what works. An important factor is to choose how and when to take these approaches with people. Be aware that sometimes joking 'with' one person may look quite harsh to someone else who's witnessing the interaction, so I avoid some public settings if I think bystanders might feel the need to step in. When people interrupt before the person has a chance to 'take the bait', they will commit it to memory as a time when they needed rescuing.

Provocative encounters don't always have to be enjoyable (in fact, there are some instances where a strongly negative response will be more helpful), but you should be very careful with how you deal with people's emotions. You need to calibrate them, be caring, and judge when to step it up (to fight back, people often need to be pushed further) and when to back down and find another way, or time, to challenge them to assert themselves. Always seek to leave people in a better state than when you found them.

Do this:

Have a crack at it

Before deciding whether or not this Provocative Style stuff is right for you (or right at all), have a go. Every time I've presented these ideas to any individual or group, I've faced some serious resistance. It's natural, it sounds scary. I think our desire to be 'nice' and not be 'mean' makes us think that being direct and joking with people about their probelms is the 'wrong' thing to do and we 'should' not do it.

When I get people to try it, they laugh and shriek and their ideas about 'right' start to bounce and jiggle around; soon they're so excited, they can't contain themselves. You understand the idea, and before we get into the techniques, have a go. The next time someone talks about a problem with you, encourage them to laugh at it and notice the effect.

Establish your rules of engagement

Chapter Twelve

When we meet people and start building a relationship with them, we test one another and establish what I call our rules of engagement. There are people in our lives who complain to us, people who are supportive and friendly, people who always ask for advice, and people who have some huge problem that they need to talk about. These will establish themselves early, and often continue to play out until one of them grows tired of it or dies. Provocative Style offers you a way to set and maintain rules mindfully, with humour, leaving you with strong, fun and mutually supportive relationships.

Recall the list of patterned behaviour, hopefully just reading it reminds you of some people in your life and how annoying that behaviour can be. Perhaps you recognised some of your own patterns. Now, we'll look at some ways of challenging those kinds of patterned behaviour, to set your rules of engagement, comparing the way it's 'normally' done, and why, in some cases, a Provocative approach works better than what we feel we 'should' do.

Blurt feedback

It's difficult to change the rules once the game is in play, so be mindful to set your rules of engagement early in the relationship. Blurting feedback lets people know you're attentive to their behaviour, and honest about your thoughts. You'll find we really enjoy knowing where we stand with people.

Frank famously had a new client come to see him who was seriously obese. The client had barely waddled into the office before Frank exclaimed 'My goodness, the Goodyear blimp has slipped it's moorings.' Again, that's quite extreme. In work environments it might make sense to avoid harsh judgements, particularly regarding physical appearance, but there can be similarly shocking observations, often about behaviour, that people will benefit from hearing. It requires courage, caring and honesty.

Blurt feedback at people. Let impulses come into your mind and rush straight out of your mouth without your brain having a chance to stop and inspect them properly. It is the offensive thoughts, flashes of insight and strange connections that your rational mind usually self-censors which are the funniest, most insightful, and often the most useful. Follow your instincts. Particularly focus on behaviour and things we can change in the moment. If someone is being noisy or obstructive, simply pointing that out (particularly as a joke or as a barbed compliment: 'What a set of lungs!') can often be enough to change the behaviour. It's certainly preferable to letting the annoyance continue until it's become infuriating because by then the way you 'mention' it will be wholly different. Compliment people. Tell them when they do or say something well, are particularly thoughtful, perceptive, kind or clever.

Blurt in meetings! If you're worried about saying something stupid, remember this: the stupidest thing to say is nothing at all. If you do say the 'wrong' thing (in truth, it's rare), then clarify what you meant, apologise if necessary, and learn from the experience. Mistakes are easy to get over, it's regret at having not done something that lingers. Focus on doing things *well* rather than getting them *right*. Right can be done only one way (see 'should'), whereas something can be done well a multitude of ways.

Point out patterns provocatively

Consider people who rejoin conversations with 'No' or 'Yeah, but...' or 'I know'. It's annoying. It's difficult to brainstorm or problem solve with those people, and they are toxic within creative environments. We usually let it continue for a while but once we've noticed it, every time we hear it, we get that little bit more annoyed. Eventually, we'll either start bitching about that person behind their back, or wait until it's 'too much' and explode at them. These are not effective strategies.

As soon as you notice that it's a pattern (I'd recommend waiting until they've done it three times), point it out, non-judgementally, with just facts and no interpretations:

- ✗ **Don't take the gentle approach (has no happy chemicals):** 'I've noticed, a few times recently, (with examples) the first word out of your mouth is "no".'

- ✔ **Do take a provocative approach (now with added happy chemicals):** 'The first thing you say when you hear an idea is 'No'. I imagine you as the No Monster, a little bit like the Cookie

Monster.' **Then sing** 'No, no, no. Every idea is a bad idea', perhaps in the tune of Cookie Monster's '*C is for Cookie*' if you know it. **The more bizarre the better.**

If it's light-hearted, the next time they say 'No', it'll be met with laughter, even if it wasn't that funny initially. This recurring laughter will now give them ongoing feedback from the group, and allows everyone to deal with the issue from a happy state. The No Monster will develop an awareness about their behaviour, which, when coupled with the useful experience of finding it funny, will offer them different ways of reacting. You may find that the behaviour continues, but differently – perhaps they'll occasionally say yes, or if they do have to say no, they'll say something like 'I hate to be the No Monster on this, but...' This is more manageable, and makes for a more creative and friendly environment.

Reward good behaviour

Set high standards, and be readily impressed. Decide what you'd like from others; whether that's humour, smart thinking, initiative, thoughtfulness, obedience or honesty, and reward it when you see it. Your level of excitement will indicate how well they're doing at impressing you. They want to be seen as honest, friendly, funny or smart, so they'll keep doing it.

→ **Drop clues** about the kind of behaviour you appreciate. In most cases, it's as simple as stating it.

→ **Reward it** when you see it. Sparkle your eyes at them. Laugh. Compliment them (in front of others). Touch them on the hand or elbow, while you:

→ **Express why you like that behaviour.** Focus upon what is impressive *about them* for doing that (not just why it makes you happy). This will fan their flickering desire to live up to your standards.

Be obvious. Seek to be impressed. Compliments are particularly important because they serve both as a hint about what behaviour you like, while rewarding that behaviour. It's a nice, honest and effective way of building a solid relationship. Tell them the following.

- ✔ 'That was nicely said.'
- ✔ 'You worked very hard on that, thank you.'
- ✔ 'You look fantastic.'
- ✔ 'You're quite funny.'
- ✔ 'That's quite perceptive.'

Punish bad behaviour

A simple and effective way of rebuffing bad behaviour is to simply say (or communicate in some way) 'No, I won't accept that.' Be firm, and be clear that it's a behaviour that is being rejected, rather than the person. Warmly accept the person again when they've changed their behaviour. Your anger is a part of you. It is only 'bad' if it's unhelpful. Those who are not mindful of it are ruled by it, and then it is almost always unhelpful and spreads like a contagion as they inflict it upon others. In those moments, breathe, and get pragmatic. Will being angry fix this? If it will (and sometimes it will), rage on. If it won't, then start focusing on solutions. If someone's trying to upset you, remember that people only seek to upset others when they are upset themselves. Find out why they're upset and fix it. Have some compassion, and rise above the gravitational pull of perpetuating the problem. Defuse the situation (perhaps with humour) and focus your mind on funny, happy, outcome-oriented things by talking about them.

In some situations, people will push your buttons. They will do it because they can, they'll do it to test you, and sometimes they'll do it because they just never thought about it. You may need to stop them and let them know, so that they do think about it next time.

Get angry if you must, but be happy again afterwards

Everyone can get angry quickly – that's not very impressive or useful – but becoming happy again quickly is rare, valuable, and quite difficult to do. Most people sulk and mutter for a while. The depressingly unimpressive can let one careless comment ruin their whole day, which will slither out from them and interfere with the happiness of others. Only when you can master your emotional state, can you indulge your darker side. When someone exhibits behaviour you will not abide, and you've exhausted a variety of more reasonable responses, snap at them – just be sure to become happy again.

→ **Speak from your gut.** You may need to raise your voice (try to avoid it), but don't shout. The chest breathing and a rough voice will make you more likely to lose it and get unmanageably upset.

→ **Be clear on your reasons,** state facts (rather than interpretations).

→ **Clearly and firmly state what you want:** 'Do not, ever, speak to me like that.'

→ **Don't go on a tirade.** Say your bit and be silent. Let them think.

→ **They will apologise** because you're speaking so commandingly from your diaphragm, you've presupposed that they will understand your anger, and you've been so lovely to them until now.

→ **Snap back to happy.** Immediately smile, relax, and start speaking nicely again. Accept their apology warmly, without excusing the behaviour. It will take a few moments longer to get your body under control (waiting for that adrenaline to wash away).

→ **Talk about pleasing things now** and you'll calm down more quickly.

→ **Do not apologise for getting angry.**

→ **Do not re-explain why you were upset.** It doesn't matter, and will get in the way of becoming happy again.

→ **If they don't apologise,** you've got some thinking to do. Were they really in the wrong? Try to see it from their perspective. Understand the influences acting upon them. If they don't hold the same values as you, then they don't hold the same values as you. That's nothing to get angry about – you simply have to decide whether you can accept them, change them, or move on. Extracting yourself from a relationship (professional or otherwise) is a serious choice you must consider, but you should do so when you're thinking properly, not while you're angry.

You are not manufacturing the anger. Both your anger and subsequent acceptance must be genuine, you're just displaying them deliberately. There is a limit on how effective this is, which is set by how often you get angry. If you sulk or get angry quite often, you're getting angry too easily. You're the problem. It isn't going to be effective unless you're rarely bothered, genuinely nice when you're nice, and until now you've been really, really nice.

Use the experience of release to learn how to quarantine your emotions. If you had a bad day at work, don't bring it home. If you're having a tough time with a client, don't take it out on a workmate. You do not *need* to talk about what's bothering you. Talk about something exciting or amusing instead. There is a physiology attached to this kind of control and release. Recognise it and nurture it. The following exercise is another one aimed at helping you let go. I first learned this method as a rite of passage into my theatre course at university, and I've since read that its effectiveness has been supported in multiple scientific studies.

When you've completed the exercise, allow yourself to adopt the physiology, chemistry and emotion that comes with letting go – and moving forward with newfound freedom.

Do this:
Practise letting go

Write about a past grievance, something that upset you and in some way still affects you negatively. This should be something that you'd like to let go and as such, should be an issue for which the time for making amends has passed. Write about what happened and how it made you feel, focusing on the negative impact it has had upon your life, and the ways in which those feelings hold you back even today. Write this out by hand, on a single piece of paper.

Burn it.

Dodge dodgy gambits

As with any system that has rules, even the loose and unpredictable rules of social propriety, people will exploit them. Some exploit asking for advice to get attention and sympathy from others. Their desire for sympathy over solutions causes perpetual advice-askers to describe their situation as unfixable, to ignore the advice, or take active steps to sabotage themselves, rendering the advice-giver incapable of doing anything except get exasperated. Compliment fishing works in a similar way. When you dodge these gambits, you're guessing at their intended outcome, and when you've decided that it's no good for either of you, you're choosing a way to respond that specifically avoids that outcome.

'Yes, and...' with the compliment fisher

Agree with people's damning self-assessments. There's no point arguing. If they say they can't do something, or that they're terrible, smelly or dumb: they know best. Agree with them and add to it. Give them some extra reasons why they can't do it, with some made-up research or reference to something preposterous like astrology. The additional reasons you create can be so exaggerated that they want to argue against them, or so strange that at the very least, they laugh.

- ✗ **Don't argue (invites them to argue against you):** 'No, you're not useless. They just haven't appreciated you for your greater qualities.'

- ✔ **Do accept and add (incites them to argue against you):** 'Yep, you're useless. If you were a farm dog, you'd have been taken out the back and shot months ago.' You can even act it out. **(It must be said with love, a nudge and a smile!)**

By accepting and exaggerating someone's pattern, they will often recognise their own absurdity and laugh. The positive physiology of laughter (which is like nodding on steroids) will lead them back to a more workable mindset. When they use that happy place to explain why the situation is not that dire, they must hear themselves say that, and will be bound to those positive words by a social contract.

This 'Yes, and' game is a rule of improvised theatre. It's also a useful rule for life: agree with people, wholeheartedly, more often. When people present new ideas, agree with them. Don't just find reasons *why* they'll work, but come up with ways to *make* them work. Nit picking is bloody annoying and doesn't get anyone anywhere. If the idea is bad: firstly, it wasn't yours, so you can relax. Secondly, you can still say yes, then your 'and' can change it. You'll encourage others to accept it and add to it, until all the additions have turned something ridiculous into something that works.

Do the opposite

When I run workshops, it's easy to notice who speaks last. Instead of doing what I think I 'ought', which is to give them the feedback, equip them with skills and gently encourage them to speak up, I've found it's actually more effective to do the opposite, and close down opportunities for them to speak. Every time they open their mouths, I'll interrupt them or say 'In a moment', or 'We're moving on to something else now.' It soon turns into a bit of a game. Once they start playing, and start butting in and speaking up, I'll let them bathe in the enjoyment of having done so, hearing the feedback from their peers: 'It's nice to know you've got a voice!' It's more fun, and much more effective than what I used to do.

Many of us spend our initial moments in a new environment (workplace, culture, social group), agonising over what we 'should' do, keenly observing the behaviour of everyone around us, desperate to find out how to fit in. Once we've become adept at following these imaginary rules, we become the enforcers of them. We do it all without ever asking 'Is this getting me what I want?'

Ask that question of yourself more often. Don't get caught in the process and lose sight of your purpose. Continually ask yourself 'What do I want?' When you're in a situation that isn't getting you what you want, particularly one that seems recurrent, try boldly doing exactly the opposite of what you'd ordinarily do.

→ If you usually listen quietly, try shouting.

→ If you usually apologise and sulk, try thanking someone and smiling.

→ If you usually compliment someone, try criticising them.

→ If you usually criticise someone, try complimenting them.

→ If you're usually quiet, try serenading people while dancing around them, sprinkling hole-punch paper confetti in their hair.

Ridiculous suggestions for the advice-asker

We often suffer from 'this or that' thinking, which is unnecessarily dualistic: 'I either put up with my mean boss, or quit and find a new job.' It's a natural part of the brain reducing its cognitive load. Unfortunately, our propensity to focus on the more worrisome outcomes often means that we're considering the two worst available options. Ridiculous suggestions release people from that problem, forcing them to consider a wider range of more reasonable options.

Ridiculous suggestions offer a fun way to step out of the frame of complaining together, *with* someone (it's called co-rumination, and it is very, very bad for both of you). There's something strangely empowering about setting your rules, and saying with your actions 'I'm here with you, but not like that.'

When people ask for advice and argue with it, or are inclined to say 'I've tried *everything*', or never follow advice but always return to ask for more, offer them ridiculous solutions. Rattle through a list of things to see if they really have tried them all, from the mundane to the ridiculous:

→ 'Become a birthday clown.'

→ 'Hire a contract killer.'

→ 'Become a hermit and move to the forest. Then you'll never have to talk to stupid people.'

→ 'Keep doing whatever you're doing' (including reasons to do so).

When the suggestions are ridiculous enough, they'll be funny. This will shift the person's mental chemistry, elevate them, and allow them to see the problem from a happy place, which is often more solution oriented. You should intentionally avoid useful answers, so that they can come up with the ideas themselves and feel ownership over them, making them more likely to follow them (that, plus useful answers are typically not very funny).

Note: Don't get *too* obsessed with making people find their own solutions, sometimes people just need advice. Use this only to avoid the seductive pull of being 'the one who fixes things' (which can often encourage a cycle of dependency in both of you), and as a method to challenge people's behaviour *only when it is patterned or counter-productive.*

Teach leadership: create problems, not solutions

It's a well-known phenomenon, and as a leader of people it's important to remember: people are infinitely more motivated to put effort into solutions that they found for themselves. Some encourage people to find their own solutions by continually asking questions. It can be effective when done skillfully, but it's a little bit boring. Don't solve the problem. Make it worse.

- ✗ **Don't ask clean questions (effective but boring):** 'And what is it about that?/And what kind of X is that X?/In what way?'
- ✔ **Do take a Provocative approach (so dirty):** 'Wow. That sucks. So you're going to be made redundant. Find a spot on the corner where I can pass and I'll drop you a few copper coins each morning. Look at the bright side, without a warm house and regular food, you'll lose a lot of that weight and won't have to shower any more.

When your advice is literal and logical, they will match that, take it seriously, be less likely to laugh, and more likely to feel disempowered and 'up against it'. By making the problems huge and silly, the story will be quite funny; allowing the listener to at least stop feeling that choking grip of worry. From there, they will be able to pose solutions, or just develop the fortitude to deal with it, because let's face it: some problems can't be fixed. Accepting the situation and letting them laugh will help them to see it differently.

'Create problems' also means: let people make mistakes, and not just because they're funny. You'll *remember* if someone says 'make sure you oil it beforehand or it'll catch fire'. If the damn thing catches fire, you'll *learn it*. When you're teaching someone the art of leadership, occasionally drop the reins or stuff it up a bit, and watch them lead.

And when you're out to get that leadership position, constantly assume that's what's going on.

Do this:

Be a really bad coach

When someone next complains to you of a problem, ask if you can 'try something new'. Say you read about it in a book by some guy if you want. Tell them you're going to be absurd and rude, just to see if it'll help with their problem.

When (if?) they agree, be the worst coach you can possibly be:

→ Interrupt them (particularly while they initially describe the problem).

→ Comically mis-hear things 'I'm sorry, did you say penis?'

→ Talk about sex, death, and money.

→ Give them advice – really, really bad advice.

→ Suggest that they're incapable of fixing it because they're incompetent.

→ Tell strange stories, the less useful and relevant, the better.

→ Continually return to ask what the problem is again.

When you finish, ask what they thought of the whole experience. Ask what they thought of it as a coaching technique, how they feel, and what they now think about their problem. (Usually, they think it's a terrible technique, but they'll have a totally new perception of their problem, and sometimes a renewed passion to fix it.)

Sustaining your momentum

Chapter Thirteen

Teaching is a remarkable thing, it's one of the few interactions between humans that is greater than win-win. Great teaching inspires curiosity, and continues to develop both teacher and student after they've parted ways. It's remarkable how teaching a skill will often help you understand it and master it more fully. My challenge to you is this: when you find a moment where a friend or co-worker complains of lacking confidence, of being misheard or not being heard at all, take a moment and teach them some of the skills you've learned here. Take this as an open invitation to do this with every skill you know, throughout your entire life. Always be teaching and learning.

Learning is a life-long journey, something that's so often repeated it's become trite. But it's true. Learning new skills is a strong defence against depression because it constantly leads from a feeling of being lost, to gaining a footing, and then climbing steadily towards skillfulness. The setting and achieving of goals, and increased comfort in expanding your realm of competence is the surest way to become happy and more confident. Exercising your brain, constantly building these neural pathways, will keep it young and may help stave off problems like dementia and Alzheimer's. It gets even better if these new skills come with a bit of fitness, fun and social interaction.

Perhaps the most valuable part of learning new skills is how new insights and methods of doing things can sneak into other areas of your life. Learning (particularly skills, but also knowledge) is cross contextual. You'll find that a trick you learned doing one thing will help you crack a puzzle in another area of your life, and that certain skills come with whole methods of thinking. Learning how to cook is great for feeding yourself, but it's also a great way to learn how to manage your time; learn about physics and chemistry; and even discover little tricks for how to open things, clean things or seal them again. Learning to fix motorbikes gave me a procedural way of thinking, of developing hypotheses, and ways of isolating faulty parts, repairing or replacing them, testing them, and putting everything back together. It has proved useful for when the computer breaks, but has also helped me in areas of my life which I had not predicted, such as debating contentious topics and fiddling with faulty reasoning. Pulling apart an argument, finding the bit that doesn't work, fixing it and putting it back together for someone is an quite effective way of exposing new ways of thinking to them. I learned those skills from apprenticing myself to a nearly illiterate mechanic in Nepal for a few months.

Speak for Yourself

We're reaching the end of this rather delightful journey. Despite my best efforts, I'm going to assume there were a few exercises in this book that you've skipped over. Perhaps you thought 'I'll do that later' or 'I already know that', or 'Yeah, like hell.' Even if you did them all, when work pressures and long-term relationships pull and tug you to conform to your previous self, old patterns will sneak back into everyday life. To sustain your development, and to develop your skills beyond those found in these pages, you must teach your skills to others.

Do this:
Teach a skill to someone else

Choose two exercises or ideas within this book and teach them to someone else. They can, if you choose, be to the same person or two different people.

The two skills should be different: one should be something at which you are quite skilled, the other should be something you weren't too sure about or were a little reluctant to try.

You'll need to do the following.

→ Find a way to present the idea of teaching them.

→ Set aside some time to do it (rather than just casually mentioning it, really do it like it's a lesson or a coaching session).

→ Explain it to them.

→ Show them.

→ Have them try, with suggestions along the way.

→ Have them try by themselves.

→ Give them feedback.

→ Get their feedback: how useful was it?

→ Get them to teach someone else.

State your purpose

I want you to dream big. I don't want this book to just be an effective way of selling gadgets or getting a raise or just benignly 'feeling good about yourself'. If that's all you wanted when you first picked it up, then great, I hope you found it, but I implore you to look further. Create a vision for yourself. For the people around you or the whole world. Decide what it is that you care about and set yourself the challenge to make a difference. I ask you to do this, not just because I want you to, but because it'll make you even better at selling stuff or getting a raise, or doing whatever it is that you do because you'll be doing it with that purpose in mind.

Take a moment and decide what it is that you value. Start with the simple: being a good friend, making people smile, being good at what you do, but ask yourself (in a Provocative way): what would you like to have written on your grave? 'Was a good friend'? Surely not. Go bigger.

Do this:
Define your core values

Get a piece of paper and write out your core values. These are the things which really matter to you, the things you want to stand for. These are the standards that you will live by, that you will be remembered for, and will live on as your legacy.

Create a compelling call to arms

I've come to see Frank's method (along with some of my own tweaks) not as a therapy, but as a way of being, for life. After learning of his method I set about exploring ways we could implement Provocative so that instead of going from therapist to patient (a one-way, top-down approach), Provocative could spread from person to person, like a virus, with symptoms of honesty, good humour and self-confidence. I found, and indeed you will too, that being Provocative is enjoyable and it invites others to respond in kind.

People can be motivated with clever wording and congruent body language for a moment or more, but the only thing that excites lasting enthusiasm is a sense of purpose. When your words, behaviour and interesting story fade from their memory, the feeling that you stand for something, and that they are a part of something worthwhile, will remain. This is why companies create mission statements because when employees feel aligned with the values of the company, they'll stick with it, and work hard for it, through thick and thin. You must do the same. You might choose to write it out and publish it (perhaps even film it and post it online). Obviously, you don't have to, but do write it out, tinker with it until you're happy with the wording, and keep it somewhere safe.

I've been hinting at my purpose and values throughout this book, but perhaps it's time now to demonstrate my call to arms:

I believe that happiness is a noble pursuit. I think that in the search for happiness, we sometimes take short-cuts and make misguided attempts to feel good now rather than ensuring real happiness later. I suspect that organised religion and many forms of pseudoscience are symptoms of this, and I believe that they need to be opposed, vociferously and compassionately. I think that my calling within this realm is to help all people feel comfortable and confident so they may present their ideas in compelling and friendly ways, and be able to evolve their thinking as new ideas come along. With humour, they can infect people with persuasive ideas and new perspectives. Together, we will ▶

march towards, but possibly never reach, the right answers. If you disagree with my aim, in accepting that you may be right, I want you to use these same skills to state your case, vociferously and compassionately. Along the way, we will become happier, healthier, and live more enriching lives. We may inhabit other planets and perhaps other star systems. With these ideals, we may reach true immortality.

I want you to share this book, and the skills within it, with others. Talk about it, review it, give it to a friend. Spread the contagion.

That is my call to arms. You can see the structure, now make one for yourself.

Do this:

Write a call to arms

Look back at your core values. Weave them together into a personal mission statement, describing what you are, why it's important, and how you're making a difference.

Choose a cause with which everyone might not already agree (that makes it more fun).

Weave your core values and mission statement into a story designed to inspire people to follow your cause. It should include all the elements we've covered earlier in the book and finish with a clear instruction.

When you have a cause, you'll find that previous concerns are suddenly made smaller by the enormity of your task.

Index

Speak for Yourself